Our dear Mary and Scott,
 Thank you for all you do to make our lives easier and more fun. You add immeasurably to our "dance."
 God keep you always.
 Love from both of us
 Mom + Dad
 June 2017

The Dance of Life

The Dance of Life

Copyright © 2017 by Dave Knecht

All rights reserved. Except as permitted under the U.S. Copyright Act of 1976, no part of this publication may be reproduced, distributed, or transmitted in any form by any means, or stored in a database or retrieval system, without the prior written permission of the publisher.

No money or other payment has been received from any person, company or other entity in exchange for any mention or lack thereof in this book.

First Edition, April 2017

ISBN 978-0-692-82871-7

Contents

Where It All Began — 3

The Fears and Freedoms of Boyhood — 8

A Will and a Way — 19

To See the World — 36

Where to from Here? — 46

The Beginning of a Long Journey — 53

Pageantry and Profession — 68

Pulling up Roots — 77

When Pines Reach the Sky — 86

We Widen Our Circle — 94

To Serve the Present Age — 107

What's a Family For? — 117

The Fullness of Life — 127

Contents *(continued)*

Time to Volunteer   141

The World is Our Parish   153

Life is Change   161

The Last Hurrah!   170

The Dance of Life

"Life is easy to chronicle, but bewildering to practice."
– E. M. Forster, *A Room with a View*

"The life of a person is not what happened, but what he remembers and how he remembers it."
– Gabriel Garcia Marquez

Where It All Began

"The grand simplicity of the prairie is its peculiar beauty, and its occurring events are peculiar and of its own kind."
– John C. Fremont

The little community of Wimbledon, North Dakota, is NOT the tennis capital of North Dakota, nor is it famous for any other reason under the sun. But to me it was the launching pad of my dance of life, and, as any place has a large part to play in the life development of any person, the village of Wimbledon played and still plays a large part in my life.

The town owes its beginning to a man named John H. Gibson, and originally the town was called Gibson. In 1893 the official post office was established there, and the name of the town was changed to Wimbledon after Wimbledon, England.

When I was born there, almost ninety years ago, it was considered a village of about 500 folk. It had two grocery stores, a meat market, a drug store, a Doctor and a Dentist, and three thriving farm implement dealers. It's population in 2013 was listed at 217. It faces the future of all small rural communities in a state that is growing in population, where farms are getting larger, families smaller, and population is growing basically in its urban communities not only from new residents, but from the number of farm families that are leaving the farmstead and moving to town.

"Wimbledon" North Dakota is one of only two known communities in all the earth to bear that name. The world - famous one, of course, is the Tennis Capitol of the World – a part of London, England, and the scene of world-wide tennis championships. This Wimbledon is thought to have been established in the early 10 hundreds. Its name originally was "Wyman's Hill" – a village identified as being built on a small rise of land near early London.

The Wimbledon of my life was established in 1892, three years after North Dakota became a state. It was established along the route of the "Soo Line," a part of a Canadian Pacific Railway development. The name Wimbledon was given to the settlement by the conductors of the developing rail line to acknowledge their British heritage – along with other names of English origin along the line: Leal, Dazey, Courtenay, Kensal, etc.

There definitely aren't any "hills" associated with my Wimbledon. In fact, our archrival in sports, Courtenay, a few miles up the line, used to have a sport cheering song:

>Courtenay on the Soo;
>Wimbledon in the slough!

The nearest "hill" to us was known as Mud Lake Hill, a slight rise of land east of town and a slope that went down to a muddy flat, whereas youngsters we used to have enjoyable days sledding and skiing in winter. A friend of ours drove to school in an old "convertible" Model T Ford. Sometimes after school we would drive out to "Mud Lake" and do wheelies on the ice that was there.

As my Dad drove me back to Wimbledon after several weeks of Boot Camp in the Navy at Great Lakes, Illinois I exclaimed to him: "What's happened to Mud Lake Hill?" "It's where it's always been," was his reply. It isn't much of a "rise"!

My Grandfather and Grandmother Knecht came out from Wisconsin to establish a homestead about three miles south of the settlement. Grandpa Jacob Knecht was born in Switzerland, in the Canton of Zurich, between two little villages of Hinwill and Wald, in the midst of the gently rising hills building up to the mighty Alps. Two of his brothers and a sister had come to America earlier, and settled near the small village of Cochrane, Wisconsin. They founded a local dairy and creamery. Their farm was recognized through all the community by its distinctive round barn that was kept immaculately clean. The old round barn still stands.

Grandpa Knecht married a woman of German descent (Wecker) from the area, and for a time he made a living by cutting wood for the steamers that traversed the Mississippi River. He filed a claim for land in North Dakota, and farmed on that claim two miles south of the townsite until his retirement.

My Grandmother Knecht was something of an outstanding citizen in the area: mid-wife, church worker, nurse, friend of many Native Americans who traveled through the area from time to time.

My Mother's parents were of old German families in the area around the village of Leal, the Treitlines and the Christs. My Grandfather Christ was a farmer, and a breeder of excellent horses. On their retirement, they settled in Wimbledon.

 My boyhood home was built next door to my Christ grandparent's home. Both of my Grandfathers had died by the time I was two. My grandmother Knecht moved back to Wimbledon from Bismarck after she had had a stroke, so I never knew her as the great human being she was. My grandmother Christ lived next door to us. She was not a "warm" grandmother so I never really felt close to her. But the families of my grandparents, aunts, uncles and cousins, played a large part in my boyhood life.

I was delivered into this world by "Doc Wanner," an undistinguished looking, cigar chewing pudgy fellow as I remember him as a growing child. I was born at 8 o'clock in the morning of a hot summer day, August 20, 1926. I inherited two older sisters, Karen (about 5 years older than I) and Perne, (another year and a half older than Karen.).

My father was born on the farm south of Wimbledon. As a young man he was apparently quite a "dude about town" – a motorcycle riding "radical." My mother, a beautiful bride at 19, was fourteen years younger than Dad. But Dad's life had changed quite radically by the time of their marriage – for the good – through a quietly developing experience of God in his life.

Dad started working as a young man for an auto and machinery company: The Fried Company. His job was to put together Model-T Fords which were shipped from the Ford Plant in Dearborn, Michigan throughout the country. They were partly constructed. Here Dad learned his mechanic abilities, and together with Otto Krueger they formed the Krueger and Knecht Garage.

Otto had some perennial drinking problems. In those days he was known as "one of the town drunks." Looking back now I recognize that he was an addicted alcoholic, and needed help he never got.
One of the "seismic" shifts in my life happened when I was ten.

I spent a quite a bit of time at the Garage in the summer to be with my Dad, and also because a lot of "interesting" people passed that way. In a way, I liked the smell of the gas and the grease! I was at the garage one morning when Otto showed up late for work, badly hungover. My Dad confronted him, though

I remember the confrontation as being gentle. I see the scene in my mind now: Dad pulled the garage keys out of his pocket and dropped them on the floor between himself and Otto. "Otto," he said, "we can't go on this way. If you want to stay in the Garage business, then you pick up the keys and buy me out. But if you don't, I will pick up the keys and buy you out. That's the way it has to be." Well, Otto didn't pick up the keys and my Father did. So from that day my father was on his own. I recall feeling a bit of anxiety about that. This would have been about 1936, a time of severe drought and depression in the upper Midwest.

The Fears and Freedoms of Boyhood

*"The boy's will is the wind's will,
And the thoughts of youth are long, long, thoughts."
– Longfellow*

When we think of childhood, so often we think of it as one long season of fun and play. The reality, of course, is far different as we recall some of the memories of our own childhood. Although our childhood days may for the most part have been days of freedom and carelessness, there will come to mind other experiences that still haunt our memories in sometimes forceful ways.

My earliest memory was of a trip with my parents on a chokecherry picking outing to a brush patch by Baldhill Creek, some 10 miles east of town. I was probably about four or five years of age. Curious to discover new places, I wandered away from the party, and the first thing I knew I was

surrounded by unfamiliar territory and no family. I panicked and cried loudly, and my parents came rushing to see what my difficulty was. I think this was my first memorable experience of the meaning of fear.

Another moment of panic still makes me sweat as I think about it. My Aunt Edwina lived about two blocks from us, across one of the well-used streets in our little town. One of the distinguishing marks of her home was that she had a board sidewalk which my grandfather had built. Another fascinating thing about going home from her house was that there was a wooden culvert under the street I needed to cross. It fascinated me every time I saw it. On this particular day (perhaps I was nine or ten) I decided I would crawl through the culvert on the way home. I don't think I actually got far into the culvert. I tried to back out but I had a difficult time backing out of the place. I panicked, but there was nothing else to do but claw my way back out of the hole, Even as I write this I find my chest tensing up and I start sweating. I still have claustrophobic anxieties when in some tight places.

Aunt Ed's house was a wonderful place of refuge for me. When I got angry with my Mother or my sisters I would "run away from home." That should scare them! So I would go to Aunt Ed's and pour out my troubles to her. She was a good listener. Then quietly she would find paper and crayons, or something similar, and put me to work on her dining room table drawing pictures. If it were afternoon, as the day moved toward evening, she would put together a simple supper, and we would partake together. Then she would say, "Well, David, it's getting close to your bedtime. Perhaps you'd better get home before your Mother worries about you." I was ready to go. What a gift!

When my parents were married they built their home just north of Grandma Christ's home. In fact our house was built on exactly the same plan as my Grandma's. The difference was that Grandma had a bathroom; we had an outhouse in the back yard. I mentioned that Grandma Christ was not a very warm Grandma but I loved to go to visit her. She loved to garden, and had beautiful flowers all summer long. I think it was from her I learned my love of gardening. Her house always smelled so good. Looking back on it I am sure that part of it was she always had an apple hanging in her kitchen that was peppered with cloves. The aroma produced by that combination was heavenly.

Our neighborhood happened to be filled with girls, so as a small boy I had few playmates nearby. The closest was a boy a couple of years older than I, but we never spent any time together. He showed up at our house one day, and asked my Mother if David was home. He had a 22 rifle in his hands. I wasn't home, and she told Burton I was not there. He pointed the gun to the ground and pulled the trigger. We never did know what his intent was – but nevertheless I was glad I hadn't been home!

My favorite playing place, when I was alone, was the north side of our house. The grass didn't grow there, and the soil was a rather sandy loam as I remember it. I had a few small cars, rubber I think, and I would make roads, tunnels, overpasses to last me literally for hours of play. And it was always cool there. I was content to be alone

But I also remember some lonely days. I was never bored, that I remember, but I was lonely. I always wanted a brother. I would talk to my parents about that often. It was only when I was in my teens that Mother shared with me that she was unable to have more children. So, no brother!

When I started school I made friends with boys, of course, though most of my friends lived on the other side of town. Even though "the other side" was not far, to me at 5 or 6 it seemed like the other end of the world. My closest friend at that time was the son of our School Superintendent.
After a couple of years of our friendship his father moved to another town. I can still feel something of the sense of loss I felt when Bunny moved away.

Our family was very active in the Methodist church. Originally my parents belonged to a German Reformed Church. I was baptized there as an infant. When my sisters started to school my father, and several others approached the old Herr Pastor. "Pastor, we think it is time we start having Sunday School in

English rather than German." The only answer they got was a determined "Nein! Nein!" It wasn't long before the old German Church was closed. Years later my friends and I would pry our way into the vacant church building and try to catch pigeons that lived in the belfry. Eventually it was torn down.

The Presbyterian Church closed also, and its members became a part of The Methodist Episcopal Church. The Wimbledon congregation in my boyhood days was a strong, vibrant congregation.

We had our "family pew" where we worshipped regularly on Sunday mornings. Dad was a part of the Men's Club and served on the Official Board. Mother, of course, was involved in the Lady's Aid and for more years than I can remember was the "superintendent" of the Children's Department.

Mother was also very involved in the Uxbridge Homemaker's Club – and their meetings were delightful times for me. They met in the old Uxbridge School, about eight miles out of town. It had many "secret" passages, and the old hardwood floors groaned thrillingly. Other women in the Club would bring their children, and we would be able to play together while the women had their meetings. We pretty much had the run of the building with its mystical hallways. The Club would also put on an exciting Halloween night with spooks to go with it. What fun! And I can remember they always had unusual delicious lunches.

At about six years of age I acquired my first pets. One was a white cat with a black spot between his eyes. As I recall I got him from an uncle's farm. It was a dramatic experience for me when we brought him home. My Dad put him head first into a rubber boot, and performed an operation that later I learned was to neuter him. He was a good cat. He loved to sleep with me. In the winter he would come to a window over our kitchen roof and Meow loudly. I could swing the storm window open and let him in. He would snuggle down under the covers with me to keep warm. I called him "Sleepy" because he loved to sleep, as most cats do.

My other pet was a white Spitz puppy. Mother "earned him" by doing sewing for a neighbor who raised Spitz dogs. I called him by the incredibly creative name "Pooch." He was an inseparable friend. He liked to accompany me every place I went – and in our small town he was able to do that. When I was in the Navy he got hit by a car on Main Street, and my Dad had to put him to sleep. He was blind at that time, about fourteen years old. I felt a great sense of loss when I came home from the Navy and experienced the emptiness of no Pooch.

I was six when my Mother decided I could begin piano lessons. As I remember I was rather anxious to begin. The lessons were taught by Rena Lindahl, the wife of the man who ran the local lumber yard. I had purchased some boards from him for some of my childhood building projects, but I had never met his wife. But I did now. Mrs. Lindahl used HEAVY perfume. She was also well endowed on the top level. She sat me on the piano bench, and showed me the proper way to sit. Then she got behind me, and reaching over my head she showed me how to place my fingers, and explained the difference between the white and black keys. By that time I was almost passing out from the strong scent of her perfume, and the smothering of her large bosom as she reached over my head. I must have stayed until the lesson was completed but I ran home almost breathlessly. "Mother, don't make me go back again. I will do anything you ask, but don't make me go back again." Thank goodness she didn't. I did finally take a year of piano lessons in my Junior year at UND, from a very attractive, young teacher who taught piano at Wesley College. She knew how to teach piano to a very un-musical person. How I wish I would have started that sooner.

In first grade I was introduced to Declamation Contests. Each child who chose to participate would choose a reading to memorize, and at a certain time be given opportunity to say his "piece" at a public gathering. I chose to participate, so I was given a story about "Scratch, the Newsboy's Dog." It was somewhat of a "tear jerker." The teacher would give you lessons on how to present the story to an audience. Near the Spring of the year there was the "declamation contest" in the local school. We presented our "declamation" before an audience where we were judged on our presentation.

In the second grade I won First Place in the local contest, and was to go to the County Seat, Valley City, about 40 miles away, to participate in the county contest. My teacher at that time was Miss Hesch. She was a tiny woman, not much bigger than we youngsters were. As the day of departure drew near I mustered up the courage to ask Miss Hesch where I would be staying, as I knew we would stay over one night. "Oh," she said, "you'll be staying with me." That raised all the fear that a small boy could muster. How could I possibly do that! I was almost paralyzed with fear as we drove the forty miles to Valley City. What a relief to discover that she had a teen- aged brother and I would sleep in his room! Isn't it amazing how, even as adults, we can magnify our fears until we discover their source and then can deal with them?

In my teen years I memorized the Gettysburg Address and "In Flanders Field the Poppies Grow." I became a regular feature at the Memorial Day Service until I was old enough to play in the band. Then another child took my place in the program. Both of these writings move me to this day.

The house we lived in was a simple, basic house plan with a kitchen, dining room, and living room on the main floor. From the living room you could go to the upstairs level with three bedrooms. My bedroom was on the southwest corner with a window that looked out over our back yard. Since our home was near the west edge of town, I could look out my window to the "country." and from there I could hear the "shoosh – shoosh" of the simple John Deere tractor in the field on the edge of town in the Spring and Fall of the year. I could also hear and see the woodpecker that would start each early morning with sharpening his beak on the aluminum covering on the steeple cross on the Missouri Synod Lutheran Church behind us.

Our house had a massive enclosed front porch that wrapped around the front of the house and partway around the side. In inclement weather it was a great place to play.

One year, on the Fourth of July, my uncle Jack and Aunt Edna came to visit us from Bismarck. They had four children, four special cousins that we didn't see very often. As we played together it was discovered that there were at least four cap pistols in our possession. A cap pistol was a small handgun that would snap its trigger onto a small dot of gunpowder on a paper roll. The explosion was sharp and loud – and smelly from the burned powder. As you pulled the trigger the gun would continue to roll the paper for more shots to fire. We cousins started a "war" on the front porch with those pistols. It not only turned the air blue, but the acrid smell was enough to make us nauseated. Eating the picnic supper was no longer a choice that appealed to us.

When I was growing up we had no running water in the house, nor a sewer for expelling the waste. Mother baked on an old wood range in the kitchen. Bringing in water and wood became a regular part of my chore schedule. The water came from a well between Grandma's house and ours, about 50 yards away. A massive (it seemed to me then) log in the backyard was my wood chopping block.

I must say I never minded these chores. They had a dimension of excitement to them that my imagination expanded. The pump, for example, was beautiful in the winter when the water left drops that would freeze into exotic and beautiful shapes and colors. And then there was the ONE TIME excitement of finding out what would happen if I put my tongue on the cold pump handle. I never needed to try that again!

Since we had no running water we had no regular bathroom. All wash water that was carried in had to be carried out. We took turns bathing in a large tub on the kitchen floor with water heated on the old range. Since I was the last child of the family sometimes my water supply was on the short side. As a teenager I used my imagination to hoist a barrel on top of the old "two holer" toilet in the back yard. This provided water for a crude shower below. The sun heated my water during the day.

Most of the year our toilet expeditions were out to the two-holer in the back yard. My Dad did create his version of an indoor toilet in the cellar to be used in the winter. It was simple: a five-gallon bucket within a wooden cabinet. How wonderful this was in winter compared to bundling up and taking the trip outside to the "biffy." But there was the necessary job somewhere along the line when the bucket had to be emptied. That was one of Dad's chores, and he tried to do it at a time when the scent of the exiting bucket wouldn't disturb the equilibrium of the entire family. I also remember a commode in the hallway upstairs that could be used for emergencies during the nights in the winter. We did what we had to do.

After all of us children had left home the village buried water pipes and sewer pipes down our street, and Dad constructed an indoor bathroom with its own toilet, tub and shower. It was wonderful when we came home to visit.

From the time I was an infant I had my own room just across the hall from my parent's room. As a child there was no question that that's the way it was, until I started school. When some of my friends learned that I slept in a room by myself they began to raise questions: : "Aren't you afraid? Do you sleep with a light on? Aren't you scared that someone may come in to kidnap you?" Their questions raised questions in my mind that I had never thought about before. It took some time for my parents to convince me that there weren't any monsters under my bed, or that no one would come to take me away. My Mother would say, "They would bring you back in the morning."

One of the hardest thing to be as a child was that my ears stuck out – extremely so, it seemed to me. I sometimes imagined that when I walked through a doorway my ears touched on both sides. It was ridiculous, but it was very real to me. I would hold my ears against my head sometimes hoping they would stay there. My mother created caps out of the tops of nylon stockings and I would wear them at night with hopes it would make my ears grow closer to my head. As I matured, of course, my face filled out and the issue took care of itself. What fears a child's imagination can raise to invade a happy childhood.

When I was about ten a friend introduced me to stamp collecting. It started first with a contest that Jimmy Allen began. Jimmy Allen was the star of a radio program we listened to religiously. He was an air pilot so that was exciting in those days to a growing boy. The program was sponsored by the Skelly Oil Company. At Skelly Oil Stations one could collect stickers about our hero, Jimmy Allen. The trouble I had was that the nearest Skelly Oil Station was a hundred miles away, in Fargo.

My Dad did make occasional trips to Fargo as his Ford dealership was through the WW Wallwork Company in Fargo. When he would make a trip to Fargo he would always make a point of stopping at a Skelly Station to pick up a sticker for me. Eventually he convinced the station attendant that since we lived so far away from a Skelly Station perhaps he could fill my album for me. He was a gracious man.

The stamp collecting interest expanded from there into collecting US and Foreign stamps. On the back of comic books there were always offers from stamp companies that for a few pennies one could receive a packet of stamps. One of the most popular was The Mystic Stamp Company. Even the name of the Company was enticing to a child! Together with my friend LeRoy our hobby collection grew. I still have the old Scott Stamp Album from those early years. Some of the foreign countries seemed to have more exciting stamps than our country did. One set that was a particular pride of mine as an adolescent (it's still in the old album) was a set of Goya Nudes from Spain. I am not sure my parents ever knew I had purchased that set! I would save up my pennies and nickels until I had enough money to order a packet of foreign stamps. It was also a great way to learn world geography. Now some of the romantic country names of those days (Afghanistan, Iran, Azerbaijan, Syria) are very much a part of our everyday life.

In addition to the satisfaction of working with the stamps themselves there are the added benefits of learning about other nations of the world, and becoming aware of some of the significant events of our nation's history

I have continued collecting stamps through all my life since then. In my later years I expanded to collecting First Day Covers, which is an envelope with a stamp issued and stamped on its first day of issue. I had about twenty-three ring albums of First Day Covers. I eventually sold them through a stamp agency, getting "peanuts" for my investment. I had many enjoyable hours, however, with my collection. I continue to keep an up-to-date collection of new U.S issues. I fear that stamp collecting is too slow an activity for today's youth. I don't believe any of my family is presently interested in my collection when I am done with it.

A Will and a Way

"Youth is the spirit of adventure and awakening. It is a time of physical energy when the body attains the vigor of good health that may require the caution of temperance. Youth is a period of timelessness when the horizons of age seem too distant to be noticed."
– Ezra Taft Benson

It was Oscar Wilde who declared "Youth is wasted on the young." But without the bridge of the years of youth there is no way we would mature into persons with minds of our own and experiences that sometimes grow out of taking the wrong road. Overall I remember the days of my youth as happy and meaningful days.

At twelve I was taken with a group from the church to a Camp Meeting at Beulah Camp Ground near Jamestown. As I look back on this experience now, the Camp was sponsored by a very conservatively-minded group.

Our Pastor's son, LeRoy, and I had become good friends even though he was two years older than I. LeRoy had the gift of appearing innocent no matter what he did. So when we got involved in any pranks, usually of his devising, guess who got the blame? One evening during the Camp Meeting LeRoy and I decided we would skip out of the evening meeting. To make matters worse we invited two girls to go to a movie with us. We had a great time – until we returned to the Camp. Going to movies was "verboten" to begin with; to encourage two of the campers to go with us was a mortal "sin."

LeRoy's uncle, who was a very conservative Pastor, met us at the gate and gave us the "what for." Of course I was considered the one who came up with the idea.

During the Camp we had Bible classes during the day. The evenings were worship services that were meant to bring us to a commitment to follow Jesus. The service usually involved a fiery Sermon that was designed to bring us to the crevasse of extreme guilt. In the Church's history there are always those who discover that "guilt" is a tremendous motivator! This particular year there was a married couple who were part of the leadership team and who were wonderful at playing the Marimbas. Their ethereal music, of course, heightened the drama of the evening. After what seemed like the singing of a hundred verses of "Just as I am, I come." I finally surrendered. I recorded in my diary that night that I had "given my life to Jesus." I know now that in reality I had done this in a quiet way while growing up in a home where following Jesus was a part of our day-by-day living. My "commitment" at that time was more a matter of getting the Camp staff "off my back."

My involvement in our local church brings back pleasant memories, and a meaningful growth in my understanding of life lived in trust in God. I was confirmed in the Methodist Church at Wimbledon. The Pastor's manner of Confirmation was the catechetical method: you memorized the answer to the questions in the book. Pastor Meier had us memorize both the questions and the answers. When he stated an "answer" we were to give him a question! I never did understand the reasoning behind that, but of all the questions and answers we learned, I remember one:

"What is the chief end of man?" "The chief end of man is to worship God and serve Him forever." That's the most important learning of them all, I think.

The intervening years have led me down many different paths of discovery in faith, but basically I have come back to the simple faith I had as a boy. Were those who knew me then as a youth to look on my spiritual life today I think they could say, as Robert Frost expressed it: "They would not find me changed from him they knew, Only more sure of all I thought was true."

About this time a family from Jamestown moved in next door in what had been my Grandmother's house. The boys had raised rabbits, and they gave me a couple of tiny rabbits, from which I established a rabbit industry of my own.

In our back yard was a small old building. I have no idea where it came from originally; it may have been a chicken coop. This became the center of my rabbit-raising industry. I built tiers of cages in the old building. I learned a great deal about the "facts of life" from this experience. My intent was to raise rabbits, and sell them, and to build up a "treasure" of my own. The only difficulty with the idea, as I soon learned, was "who do you sell dozens of rabbits to in a small town?" I gave most of them away, making a lot of children happy, and not a few disgruntled mothers. I learned much from the experience, and enjoyed it along the way.

On this same old building was a porch. From somewhere came the idea that I could not only raise rabbits in the old building, but if I would screen in the porch I could raise pigeons. What fun, and what a learning experience. Friend LeRoy and I would go out to nearby farms, convince the farmer to let us try to catch the pigeons in their hayloft, and it worked. We had pigeons by the dozen. The mature birds made nests and laid eggs which, given care, hatched into squabs. As we watched the squabs grow we recognized that they were also delicious eating. I'm surprised we convinced our mothers it was so.

There was one experience in the whole pigeon business that stands out in my mind – another of the tectonic plate shifts in a young life. On the edge of town was an abandoned grain elevator. There were pigeons galore always circling the elevator and flying in and out of the broken windows. What a source for pigeons! So late one afternoon, my friend and I dared to go into the old elevator. We discovered there was still in existence a platform lift that once was used to take the workmen up to the different levels of the elevator. We pulled on the lift rope, and it seemed to be sound. (Angels watching over me?) We got to the level where we could walk out on the thick walls separating the grain bins below. I am not sure, but my guess is these walls were made of stacked 2 x 8 or 2 x 10 planks. The pigeons were flying in and out over our heads. In the excitement of the moment we ran on the tops of these bin dividers, reaching up to catch pigeons as they flew past. The bins were empty, and it was probably thirty feet or so to the bottom. When we went home with our catch (I do not know how many we had) we began to contemplate the stupidity of our enterprise. I still think of it occasionally, and thank God for keeping a couple of stupid kids alive.

With all of our "experience" in the pigeon business we never did discover which were males and which were females! LeRoy's Dad was not the most exciting person I knew at that age, but he had a care for youth. We had an active youth group in our church – The Epworth League. Pastor Meier started a Scout Troop as well. That led us into many exciting and wonderful worlds: camping, learning camp skills, the fellowship of the troop, a week at Camp Shawandasee in Minnesota (on a lake!) for the District Camp. There I was to meet many youth from other towns. Some of them were splendid Scouters. One boy in our cabin was green as grass. He was enamored with the clams he found in the lake.

Unbeknown to us he collected them and kept them in a pail under his cot. Obviously, it wasn't more than a day or two, and the presence of the clams made themselves known in the most horrible odor I think I have ever smelled.

Scouting meant a great deal to me. I am sorry that I was never able to convince one of my grandsons to give it a try. I had completed all of my work up through the Life Scout level, when our Scoutmaster was transferred to another church in another town. No other adult was willing to take over so our Troop was disbanded. I never was able to become an Eagle Scout. I have always regretted that to this day.

The transfer of our Scoutmaster meant that one of my friends would leave as well – his son LeRoy. Through our Junior High years there were three of us that did so many things together: LeRoy, Durward Koll, and myself. We were somewhat humorously referred to as "The Tragic Trio." We never got into any major trouble, but we certainly had good times.

Durward had a grandpa who raised potatoes. In the Fall he would hire youth like ourselves to come to his fields to pick up the potatoes he had turned up with his machine. We would fill a bucket with potatoes and dump them in sack, until the sack were full. At the end of the day the sacks would be tied and loaded on a trailer for transport to town.

One of the workers one afternoon was a friend named Oscar Henderson. Oscar was a small boy who talked with a high voice that was rather humorous to hear at times. But he was a great kid. That afternoon we all decided that we would pepper Oscar with the tiny potatoes we found, and of course he got quite a shower of them. Suddenly we heard this high-pitched voice: "Enough's enough, boys!" Our signal that perhaps we had gone a little far.

Durward's Grandpa was an interesting person. He chewed what was called "Cut Plug" tobacco, a hard chunk of tobacco so dark it looked like a piece of licorice. Grandpa Kolberg had a friend who was always hitting him up for a cut of tobacco. Grandpa got tired of this, naturally, so he devised a way of putting a stop to it. The next time the chump begged a chew Grandpa Kolberg pulled the cut plug out of his pocket and said, "Sorry. It may be a little damp. I can't hold my water as good as I used to." He was not asked for a cut of chewing tobacco again.

Durward had a little brother who for some reason took a liking to me. When he was around he would follow me like a little puppy. He was kind of a mean little guy. He would lure rabbits over to the cage wire, and then light their whiskers with a match. I often wondered what would ever happen to him.

Well, as the story progressed the boy grew up, took flying lessons and became a crop duster in the cotton country of Mississippi. He cracked up in his airplane one day, but fortunately lived and was taken to a local hospital. He was a smart lad, and while he was lying on his bed in the hospital he devised a way of moving patients from one bed to another bed or to a gurney without stress. He and a friend were able to patent the idea and they received something over a million dollars for the patent. Never sell a person short!

We had no swimming pool in our little town, and the closest lake was Spiritwood Lake about 12 miles down the road. But some of us discovered an alternative. The Midland Continental RR terminated in Wimbledon. Originally it was to run from Winnipeg, Canada to the Gulf of Mexico. The advent of the first war put a halt on building; then came the Stock Market crash in 1929; then the depression, and at last WWII. So the project was never finished. The only portion finished was from Wimbledon to Ellendale, a few miles south of Jamestown. In its final years it served as a transfer track between the BNSF in Jamestown, and the Soo Line in Wimbledon.

Hiking the tracks one day with our 22 rifles to shoot gophers along the way, 2 or 3 of us discovered that about a mile and a half out of town there was a pool of water in the RR ditch that was deep and inviting. We stripped down on the spot and discovered a neat swimming hole. It was respectable swimming until about the end of June when the water became a little greasy and smelly. It was a popular swimming hole until we learned to drive and could make the trip to Spiritwood Lake. Sometimes there would be as many as a dozen boys out there swimming in the raw.

A cousin of mine, female type, learned of this and rounded up a couple of her friends to surprise us one day. We saw them coming, but there wasn't anything we could do at that stage of things. So we watched them come. We stayed in the water, and kept the muddy bottom stirred up until they became tired of the game and took off. Sometimes, when I am in Wimbledon I am tempted to hike down the tracks again and see if the pool is still there.

In the 7th grade I was persuaded to join the school band. The Director wanted me to play a Baritone horn. I admit I tried it, but it had no romance for me. Friend LeRoy played a Tenor Saxophone so somehow the folks were able to find the money to buy me a Tenor Sax – a Buescher. It was a beautiful instrument and I loved to play it. My dog Pooch would often join me in a "duet" when I practiced at home. Apparently the music vibrations really irritated his ears. I had been playing the cymbals in the community band, and to be honest cymbals seemed like a drag to me. The saxophone had glamor to it. As

I have gotten older I have come to realize how important the sound of a cymbal can be.

With my sax I managed to play occasionally with a dance band for community dances. I am sorry to say that community dances in Wimbledon, after about 10:30 p.m. or so, were not the most pleasurable place to be. Too much boozing. So I would usually play until 10 or 10:30 and leave.

When I was at the University of North Dakota I played in the University Marching Band. That was a great experience under the very capable leadership of Dr. John Howard. Dr. Howard had the capacity to get music out of that band.

When I was at my first pastoral appointment at Fairmount-Bethany, it was the first year that Pastors had to start paying Social Security. I sold my saxophone to have enough money to pay the bill. I have wished many times since that I had explored other sources for the money and kept my sax.

On the east edge of Wimbledon was a farm that was our "local dairy." Mrs. Lewelyn was the manager. She would deliver milk in bottles to homes in the village. The tops of the bottles sloped up, and in the winter, when the milk would freeze, if we didn't get it in the house soon enough, the expanding milk would push up and out of the neck of the bottle. Free ice cream!

During my sophomore year in high school our "milk lady" asked me if I would be interested in herding her sheep through the summer months. Why not? The only difficulty was that the sheep were to be kept within the oval of the race track in the city park. There was one old buck I called "One Eye" for obvious reasons. He was never happy staying within the grass of that oval, so I was constantly on guard to keep him from leading the whole flock astray. Years later, as I became a Pastor in a local church, I often thought that this was an invaluable lesson in preparation for becoming a Pastor of a church. Now I know something of what Jesus was talking about when he referred to God as our Shepherd, and we as God's sheep! Aren't we all tempted at some time to "wander away"?

Most summers I would spend at least a week at my Aunt Em and Uncle Lou's farm. They lived about five or six miles south of town. They were such gracious people. Uncle Louie was the quiet type, never said much, but he ran deep, and my love for him was deep. I was able to tell him that just a short time before he died.

The summer on the farm exposed me to a practice I had never experienced before. One farmer had a prize stallion, and he had a buggy that he would drive around the country "servicing" mares that a farmer wanted to breed. It was quite an operation to observe certainly.

But years later, as I read a statement, by Ernest Hemingway I think, he said "every time I see a sign that says 'Service' I wonder who's getting screwed! Crude, but so often true.

Near the conclusion of my Junior Year of High School I decided I would like to get involved in the harvest process to earn some money and take some of the financial burden off my folks. Besides most of my high school friends were farm guys so this a natural thing to them. In those days, when harvest was much later than it is now, my cousin Bill and I signed up to shock grain bundles for an old farmer who lived north of town. He lived out about six miles so he suggested we just stay out overnight until the job was done.

We went out for our first day of work. Nick's wife was gone but he assured us he would see that we were taken care of, and sure enough he put together our first supper in great shape. We shocked the bundles of grain in the hot sun, quitting in the cool of the evening. In those days most of the grain was cut by a binder that would tie the sheaves of grain into bundles that would be ready for pitching into a threshing machine. But before threshing day the bundles were set together in a shock with the heads pointing up in such a way that when it rained the shocks could shed the water.

When we stopped work for the evening he showed us our bedroom, and after we'd washed off the itchy chaff from the bundles we crawled into bed. It was a hot night. We probably didn't sleep an hour before we both woke up, itching all over. At first we assumed it was the grain chaff, but Bill said "Let's take a look," so we turned on the light. As we looked at the sheets, and then around the edge of the mattress we had our answer: bedbugs. I had never seen one before so I wouldn't have known what they were, but Bill did. We got up, shook out our blanket, and went to the hallway and spread the blanket out on the floor. The old man awakened, and wondered what the trouble was. We told him we got too hot, which we had. The next day we told him that since his wife was gone we needn't bother him to arrange for us; we could go back home for the night. That we did. I think we worked three or four days before we finished the job.

The next step for me was to join a threshing "crew." The crew would move from farm to farm and field to field with a threshing machine. We were to pick up the bundles of grain on a special wagon called a hayrack, and take them to the threshing machine and toss them in for threshing. On my first day I was assigned a team of horses and a hayrack. My only familiarity was with horses was with those that were trained for riding. This team of horses was massive; it was meant for hard work. They had to be harnessed to the hayrack. I knew what a harness was, but I had never harnessed a horse in my life.

When it came time to harness up I couldn't even reach the back of the horses, let alone lift the heavy harness affair to the top of them. (I must confess I was the 120 pound weakling.) One of the men helped me get the horses harnessed and attached to my wagon.

When it was time to go out to the field I mounted my hayrack, said "Giddyup" and the horses went flying as though they knew where they were going – and maybe they did, but I didn't. We went flying through the gate out of the farmyard, and took the mailbox with me! Embarassing. But after I made it through that first day, all went well. I still couldn't harness the horses by myself, but the crew was willing to help this skinny little kid to do that job.

The plan was that when we would finish up one farmer's fields we would then move on to another farmer's fields. We were going to one that was only about two miles out of town. This was to be our last move. We were to finish up the season at Old Jim's fields. Some of the veterans of the crew warned me: "Old Jim is a tightwad. He thinks he will save money by making the bundles as large as the binder will make them. But we fool him. They are heavy, and we slow down."

They WERE heavy and as the afternoon wore on I wondered whether I could even make it to quitting time. I was about ready to throw in my pitchfork and admit that I didn't have the strength to finish the day. How could I face that kind of embarrassment? Then I spotted coming down the road toward us our old "Green Hornet." This was a vehicle my Dad had created by cutting the body off the chassis of an old Chevrolet. Dad used this "jitney" to deliver propane bottles to customers.

Driving the Green Hornet was my Dad. He had recognized that given the heat of the day, and the field on which we were working, I maybe could use some help. So he drove out to the field, picked up an extra fork and helped me finish off the day. What a wonderful feeling.

I have used this experience a time or two in talking about the Grace of God. Just when we think we can't make it on our own anymore, the Spirit of God moves in to give us the strength we need.

A favorite activity of our early High School days was horseback riding. On the east side of town was a tumbledown shack where old Bill Fredericks lived. He was an old bachelor that must have had a very checkered background. No one in town knew where he had come from originally. Together with my cousins John and Bill, we would stop by to see old Bill from time to time. I'm not sure when he had shaved last, or had a bath. But he was an interesting old fellow and he would entertain us by telling stories, some of them perhaps true; most of them obviously prevarications. We enjoyed him.

He also had a half dozen horses. They must have been old too; they were not spirited horses. He let us ride them whenever we wished to. That satisfied our desire for horseback riding. We would go into the countryside, get as much speed out of them as they were capable of, and it was a most enjoyable outing for us

While my Dad was still in the Garage business he also sold cars – used cars, and new Fords. Dad was a Ford man until the day he died. When every other automobile company came out with hydraulic brakes Ford still insisted on producing mechanical brakes. Dad stuck to the Ford mantra: "From wheel to wheel a band of steel."

Dad had taken in on trade one time a 1936 Lincoln Zephyr. The Lincoln Zephyr was quite a car. I have no idea where it had come from. The Lincoln, then as now, was considered a luxury car. The interior was exquisite. It was an awesome sight to a teenager to lift up the hood on that car and see this twelve cylinder power house. What power! Of course it had mechanical brakes.

I persuaded Dad to let me take the Zephyr to Spiritwood Lake one hot summer day. There were at least four of us, although I can't remember who was along. All went well until we came to the lake. There was quite a steep hill (for North Dakota) going down to the swimming beach, but we started down. The Zephyr kept going faster and faster, and I discovered the brakes would not stop it. What now? I laid on the horn to warn people, and luckily swimmers got the message in time to get out of the way. I drove down to the edge of the lake, and turned it sharply to go back up the hill, and finally I was able to get it stopped. When I got home I said, "Dad I'll never drive this old brute again."

But I did. It was my Senior year. Rather than trying to have a Senior Prom (there were 14 of us in the class) we decided we would have a dinner and theater party in Jamestown. The father of one of the girls, T.A. Morrow, agreed to take a load to Jamestown in his brand new Plymouth. I agreed to take a carful of youth as well. There was a third car but I can't remember who was driving it.

 I was following Mr. Morrow in the Lincoln. Suddenly he saw his grocery supply truck coming toward him and wanting to give the driver a message Mr. Morrow stopped right in the middle of the highway. I couldn't stop. I couldn't go outside of him because the ditch was too deep. I couldn't pass him or I would crash into the truck. I pushed on the brakes with as much pressure as my skinny legs could muster, but the inevitable happened. I slammed into the back of Mr. Morrow's new Plymouth. Fortunately no one was hurt. The grille on the old Zephyr was pushed in. The Plymouth was not damaged that much. Mr. Morrow realized he had done a rather stupid thing, so everything came out reasonably well. I didn't drive the Zephyr again, because shortly after that I graduated from High School and left for the Navy.

There is one last experience to share from these High School days. It was in my Junior Year. I wanted to earn some extra money to buy clothes for my Senior Year. I signed up to sell Cosmopolitan Magazines. I had actually worked up a pretty good route of customers.

One of the extras of the experience, besides earning money from selling the magazines, a person could also accumulate points that could be exchanged for extra "prizes." One of the teachers I had in chemistry was such an excellent person. I practically worshipped the ground he walked on. I decided I would earn an extra gift to give him for a Christmas gift, and the best idea seemed to be a canary. So I worked like a fool, and I got the canary.

The teacher and his wife took off for the Christmas holidays. I figured I would wait until he came back to town and then have the satisfaction of giving him this special gift. Christmas happened.

I took care of the canary in the meantime. I returned to school after vacation was over to learn that he had left our school system and had accepted a teaching job somewhere else.
It was a real heartbreaker – perhaps the first major disappointment in my young life. I had the first canary in my life.

Drop back a few years to 1941. My friend LeRoy and I were lying on the living room floor at his home listening to their old massive stand-up radio, when suddenly programming was interrupted and the announcement was made of the Japanese attack on Pearl Harbor. LeRoy had one more year of High School to go; I had three. We knew that years of war might be ahead. We talked about what our futures might be. Both of us recognized that the war would probably continue long enough to include us.

"Well," LeRoy said, "I'll go to the army. At least I'll have some ground underneath my feet."

Romantic as I was at that time my reply was something like this: "I think I will choose the Navy. I think it would be great to have the experience of the sea, and also to have the chance to visit other lands of the world."

As it turned out, both of us ended up where we had decided that day we wanted to be.

This must be said before I go any further. School athletics are an important part of small town life. Athletic abilities were not in my birth gift pack. To this day I am not particularly coordinated. The only high school athletic activities in our town in those days was basketball and track. I did envy my friends who were athletic. I tried out for Grade School Basketball. Mother had made a pair of shorts by cutting off a pair of jeans. I had never even heard of an athletic supporter! But the closest I got was to warm a spot on the bench.

I never even tried to join the team in Senior High, but I did end up as the Manager of our Basketball Team and I thoroughly enjoyed that. The unsettling thing at this place in my life is the recognition that most of the boy athletes in my class died ten to fifteen years ago. And this old clutz is still around. But I am grateful.

Romance, too, was not a great part of my life. I suppose for one thing the choice of young women in a small school like ours was not great, nor their choice of young men. I did have one attraction for a girl that perhaps lasted a year – enough to get some teasing from my friends. But it certainly wasn't a profound romantic relationship!

I shall always be grateful for the opportunity to grow up in a small town. We certainly didn't have a lot of the opportunities that my grandchildren have had, growing up in larger cities. But not knowing of them we didn't miss them. Looking back we weren't ever bored, as so many youth seem to be today. There was always something that we found interesting to do or to get involved with. The number of relationships possible in a small community still gave us a taste of a larger life that seemed to be sufficient. There was a stabilizing force to all of our activities. Everyone knew whose child we were, and although there may have been times that was somewhat restrictive, it also kept us from getting into any serious trouble. After all I was "Herman's boy" no matter what I did in the community. That was a source of pride to me because my family was respected by most if not all in the community.

My parents were wise in our upbringing also. They drew lines, but they also lived by "grace." I knew how they stood on various behavior issues and I never pressed them. My Dad, in his wisdom, would never give me a lecture about what I should or shouldn't do. When I left the house he would simply say, "David, remember who you are." It was enough.

To See The World

"You must know that there is nothing higher and stronger and more wholesome and food for some good life in the future than some good memory, especially a memory of childhood, of home. People talk to you a great deal about your education, but some good sacred memory, preserved from childhood, is the best education. If a man carries many such memories with him into life, he is safe to the end of his days." – Dostoyevsky, The Brothers Karamzov

In January of my Senior year of High School a Naval Recruiter out of Jamestown came to our school and offered the boys in the class an opportunity to take a test for Radio Technician. If we passed we would enter the Navy as a Seaman First Class rather than an Apprentice Seaman. I don't remember that anyone else in the class took the test but I did, and I passed it handily. My only barrier was my eyesight, and I managed to squeak by that one. I was only 17 at the time. I went to Jamestown and was accepted into the U.S Navy. I was told that on September l, after I turned 18 on August 20 , I was to report for duty at the Naval Recruiting station in Fargo for transportation to Great Lakes Naval Training Center.

And so began another epoch of my life, another shifting of the tectonic plates that shaped the boundaries of my life. Another tune to dance with.

When the day arrived, my parents took me to Fargo to report in for duty. I had never been away from home for any length of time – perhaps a week or so at the most. So it was a wrenching experience for me to say goodbye to my Mother and Dad. There were only five of us men in the group as I remember: a boy from Grand Forks, a boy from Dilworth, and I have no idea where the others were from.

We were sworn in, and at the proper time taken to the Railway station where we boarded for travel to Great Lakes. I had never ridden on a train before, so this in itself was an adventure. I had to explore the train from one end to the other. We went as far as Minneapolis, our first stop. The details of that stop are fuzzy to me but we were taken to the base at Fort Snelling for our physical examination and admission.

The first order was to remove ALL of our clothing and place them in a bag which would then be sent to our homes. So there we stood, "naked as a jay bird" as the old saying goes – a mass of humanity of all sizes, shapes and descriptions. The physical, as I remember it, (stoop over!) was somewhat dehumanizing, but we continued down the line. Then at a particular point we who were going to the Navy were shuttled off to the side, and little by little they threw into a basket our shoes, socks, and Navy uniforms, and we were given a chance to dress. I remember feeling rather weird, but also proud, as I experienced being in uniform for the first time.

We were bussed to a hotel for housing for the night, another first experience in my life. Early in the morning a bus was in front of the hotel door, to take us to the rail station for transport to Great Lakes. We were now treated as raw recruits with every move ordered. For me it was a mix of anxiety and excitement, wondering what the next step would be.

Upon arriving at Great Lakes we were assigned to a Company (mine was #1758) and marched (?) to the barracks that was to be our home for the next seventeen weeks. Our Company Commander was a Petty Officer 3rd Class, from the Boston area. As we got to know him he was a laid back fellow, very friendly, and he understood perfectly the initial anxiety that some among us were experiencing.

He gave us an overview of what the next weeks would mean. There were a lot of things to be learned about Navy life. We were expected to wash our own clothes. They were dried on lines in the laundry room, and then were to be rolled, and tied tightly in the roll with small cords and kept in our sea bags. The sea bag was a large canvass bag which hung on a rail down the center aisle of the room. Our orders for the "uniform of the day" were given to us first thing in the morning of each day. We had "blues," "whites," and "dungarees." We marched everywhere we went. We were expected to stand "god" duty in our turn. It took me a while to catch on to what he was referring to as "god" duty. I learned soon enough. With his Boston accent he was speaking of GUARD duty!

The bathroom was called "the head." It was a long room with about 20 toilet stools on one side (no partitions of course). Down on the end of that row of stools was one that had a sign over it: "FOR PERSONS WITH STDs. " That had to be translated for me: "For persons with sexually transmitted diseases." I never saw it used. I was tempted to use it one time to see what the reaction would be. My guess is it was the cleanest stool in the entire place. The showers were on the other side of the Head. There were 15-20 shower heads where we took mass showers. We had one young fellow who wouldn't take showers for some reason or other. Our guess was that he was uncomfortable being naked among so many men. Obviously modesty didn't last long around there. His unwillingness to take a shower became a problem after a while, and so some of us took it in hand by man-handling his clothes off, carrying him into the shower, and scrubbing him down with a kiyi brush (the brush we scrubbed our clothes with!). As I recall he began to take showers from that point on.

In the morning we had to make our beds tight enough so a coin would bounce when thrown on top of it. Smoking could be done only when "the smoking lamp is lit." Cigarettes were free! Why not smoke? (The tobacco companies knew what they were doing.) When I started college I changed to a pipe. When the pipe got so "strong" I couldn't stand it anymore I gave up smoking completely, and have been thankful ever since.

One of the boys developed an infection of his penis and had to be circumcised. It apparently was a very painful experience at that age so for those of us among the uncircumcised it became a vivid lesson on the importance of cleanliness! To be honest with you, up to that point, the word "circumcision" was not a part of my North Dakota vocabulary.

A new young man from South Carolina came into our Company about two weeks into our duty. His story was that the dentist had slipped and run a drill through his cheek, so he spent some time in the dispensary. His name was Robert Hood, from Rock Hill, SC. "Hood" (we often spoke to one another by our last names) and I became good buddies, and continued our relationship through many years until he died at the age of 82. He was a "died in the wool" rebel until the day he died, but we enjoyed each other's company. He could never understand anyone living in the far northland. I often said, "Bob, you don't really get the thrill of the change of seasons because your year just slides from one season to the other. Besides, thirty degrees below zero keeps out the riffraff." His full name reveals the depth of his love of the south: "Robert Jackson Hood."

My bunk was between two Jewish boys: Koeppel and Koplowitz. This was my first experience of a person of the Jewish Faith, and I will be forever grateful. They were fine young men, and brilliant. We used to get invited with them from time to time to Jewish weddings in Milwaukee. After all, young men were scarce. The rich foods of the wedding table were out of this world.

The days were full: marching, washing clothes, learning to tie knots, serving guard duty, washing clothes, marching, learning to fight oil fires, guard duty, washing clothes, marching, chow duty……..you get the idea. It was a great growing -up experience. I value it yet. After the "graduation" ceremony we were given a week of leave. I had to take a train from Chicago to Minneapolis, and wait over a day (because I slept through my first chance to catch the Soo to Wimbledon) and then the same trek back to Great Lakes where we were to be reassigned.

We were recruited to be Radio Technicians, and were granted a Seaman First Class rating, two pay grades above the newly enlisted Apprentice Seaman. Our Company was scorned and berated by other Companies as we passed them on the parade ground because of our special rating. But we could take it.

The Radio Technician School was located at 3711 West Douglas Boulevard on the west side of Chicago. It was a small city Junior College, Herzl Junior College, that had been leased to the Navy for electronics training. The school was later re-named Malcom X College, and moved to a different part of the city.

The school provided comfortable housing, although pressed for space. As I remember it, it had a lot of steps and through the day we moved from one level to another, so we got exercise. The first two or three weeks were pretty basic theories of electronics. Then we moved into advanced math, using logarithms and slide rules, all unfamiliar to me. We went to school from 8 a.m. to 10 p.m.

As I re-read some of the letters I wrote home from there I was tired all the time. There were several of us who had a real struggle to keep up. As we discovered each other we decided we would deliberately flunk out of there and be re-assigned, although they threatened that we would be sent immediately to the Sea Bees for training in Louisiana and on to the combat zone.

Somehow I was released from the training program even though when I left the school I had excellent marks. I was sent back to Great Lakes for reassignment. While waiting for reassignment I spent many hours in the chow hall – working. Actually it was good duty. Our group made friends with the chief cook. After the last group had left after supper we were given great treatment with steak or pork chops with all the trimmings, and all the ice cream we could eat.

That didn't last long however. In the process the Navy discovered that I could type. It was mid-1945, and by this time the government had established Separation Centers for discharging those who were eligible as the wars wound down. Typists were needed for all of these operations. I was sent over to another area for Yeoman's School to be trained in all the paper work required, learning short hand, and becoming acquainted with the discharge process.

Yeoman's School was good duty. The school days were not as long as that at Herzl. The subject matter was about things with which I was already acquainted, other than learning the names and numbers of various forms that were needed. Typing was a breeze for me as I had captured the "outstanding" level of the typing class back in good old Wimbledon High. In addition I made friends with two more men who became lifelong friends: Harold Lempke, who had been a High School teacher from Traverse City, MI, and Richard Howe who was from White Bear

Lake, MN. Harold was married and was a few years older than I. Dick was raised on a farm just out of White Bear Lake. Both of these men were men of solid religious background, and many times kept me from making a fool of myself. I kept in contact with both of these men until their death. We still communicate with their surviving families.

Upon completion of Yeoman's School I was sent for duty to a Separation Center at Gulfport, MS – my first experience of the deep south. This too was good duty. We put in our day's work, had the evenings and the week-ends off.

We spent several week-ends in New Orleans and came to love the cuisine of the area. The one hitch was that we couldn't board the train to New Orleans in Gulfport. (No sailors allowed). We had to go to nearby Biloxi, the site of an Air Force Base, to get the train.

This was my first experience of signs like: "No Colored Allowed," "Colored Rest Room," "Not Open to Coloreds."

While at Gulfport I came down with the measles and was put in Quarantine for a week or so in the Sick Bay. There was one other young man with measles in there at the same time. We were the only ones in Sick Bay so we were catered to by all of the nursing staff. As in typical Navy practice we only knew each other by our last names, so I remember his last name was "Campbell," but I have no idea what his first name was. We enjoyed each other's company. Neither of us was really ill. We played a lot of games, listened to a lot of music, drank a lot of pineapple juice – and sang a lot of songs. It was a fun time, and the days went flying by.

The Japanese had surrendered in 1945, while we were in Yeoman's School. The work at the Separation Center began to slow down, so I was again sent back to Great Lakes to be re-assigned. This time the wait seemed like a long time. I spent a lot of Chow Hall duty, not as lush as it had been before. But eventually I was assigned to the Naval Air Station at Jacksonville, FL., which was close to the Mayport Naval Base. A lot of my Yeoman's work there had to do with assignments at the Naval Base. We had an excellent WAVE in charge of our office, Chief Petty Officer Hirsch, and a lot of good men to work with.

This was supreme duty, but I became restless. I had joined the Navy to "see the sea." I made an appointment with my Commanding Officer.

When I was finally ushered in to see him, he said something to me to which I gave the wrong answer. In the Navy there are two "yes" answers: "Yes Sir" and "Aye, aye sir." "Yes Sir" is a positive yes answer. "Aye, aye sir" is a positive answer to a command. Whatever, I gave the wrong reply so had to listen to a brief lecture on that. He was sitting behind a large desk in a very large office, and his demeanor was enough to send shivers down my spine.

> "What do you want, Sailor?"
> "Sir I have been in the Navy almost two years and I have not been to sea yet."
> Loudly: "SAILOR, DON'T YOU KNOW THAT 70% OF THE NAVY IS ON LAND?"
> My meek reply: "No Sir, I didn't know that."
> CO: (Firmly) "WELL BE HAPPY WHERE YOU'RE AT!"

The end of my interview! Putting my tail between my legs I went back to my duty station.

My friend, Jack Hood, was now assigned to the Naval Base at Norfolk, VA. I went to visit him one week-end, and when I saw his quarters aboard ship I gave a quiet "thank you" to God that I was still at Jacksonville.

I was discharged from the Separation Center in Jacksonville. I hitchhiked up to Rock Hill, SC to see my friend Jack, who had been discharged earlier. Hitchhiking was no problem in those days.

If you wore your uniform the world was at your feet. There were still USOs in large cities so there was always a place to stay, to get food, and to get tickets to any special entertainment going on.

I hitch-hiked to Washington, D.C. and spent three or four days there, seeing the sights of the city, and sleeping in the USO at night. I hitch-hiked to New York City and spent three or four days there, sleeping at the USO at night. I hitch-hiked to Traverse City, MI to spend some time with Harry and his family; then on to White Bear Lake, MN to spend some time with Dick Howe and his family. As I look back on this now I wonder how a small town boy from North Dakota had the nerve to step out on his own and hitch hike alone half way across the country. But the uniform was a key to many doors.

From Minneapolis I took the train to Valley City where my parents met me, and I was back home in a small village in the flat center of the northern plains, and it felt so good to me.

In the year I turned 88 years of age one of our grandsons, Benjamin Kluver, enlisted in the Navy, and went to Great Lakes for Boot training. At his graduation ceremony we watched the whole thing unfold on our computer. As I watched I became aware that it was 70 years, almost to the day, that I had graduated from Boot Camp at Great Lakes.

Where to From Here?

"In later life as in the earlier only a few persons influence the formation of our character; the multitude pass us by like a distant army. One friend, one teacher, one beloved, one club, one dining table, one work table are the means by which his nation and the spirit of his nation affect an individual." – Richter

It was late September before I set foot again in my old home town of Wimbledon.

It had always been my intention to go to College, but where? The only college I knew anything about was Valley City State Teachers College in nearby Valley City, 40 miles from home. My sister Karen had gone there, and was now teaching school. But did I want to be a teacher? If I did, what would I teach? Here I was, within days of the start of any College or University I would choose to attend.

My friend LeRoy was just home from the army. After our talk in his living room on Pearl Harbor Day he had had one "hell" of a journey in the Army, with intensive fighting in Europe, and a lot of time in Germany. He had decided to go to the University of North Dakota in Grand Forks, and had already decided he wanted to go into Economics.

So I decided to go to the University with him, and hopefully come to some vocational choice along the way. We travelled to the University and were registered in the hoard of veterans that were now coming back to civilian life. Rooms were at a premium. We had to sleep on cots in the wide open spaces of one of the athletic buildings of the University until a room could be found. We learned of Wesley College, across

University Avenue from the University. They would have a room, after things settled down a bit, in Sayre Hall, a boys' dorm of this little college.

In 1893 the Methodist Episcopal Church had established a little school of religion in Wahpeton, ND. It was known as Red River Valley University. In 1905 the school had to be closed because of financial difficulties. The Trustees worked out an affiliate relationship with the University of North Dakota in Grand Forks. In that negotiation it was agreed that the new Wesley College would teach classes in religion, philosophy and music at Wesley College, and credit earned there would count toward a degree from UND, and vice versa.

LeRoy and I were soon settled in a suite of two rooms with two other men: Everett Matz and Harvey Augustine. Everett was aiming for the ministry; Harvey for economics.

Along the line in my growing up days my thoughts had thought of the possibility of a career in the Christian Ministry, but I had put it on the back burner. The awareness of so many young men I met in the Navy who had no sense of reason for being, somewhat haunted me, and was to become a part of my "call" to the ministry.

A familiar poem by Vachel Lindsay seemed to fit so many of these young men:

> Let not young souls be smothered out
> Before they do quaint deeds and fully flaunt their pride.
> The world's one crime is that its' babes grow dull,
> Its' poor are oxlike, limp and leaden eyed.
>
> Not that they starve, but starve so dreamlessly.
> Not that they sow but that they seldom reap.

> Not that they serve, but have no gods to serve.
> Not that they die but that they die like sheep.

I remembered with fondness my experiences in chemistry in High School., so I considered that route. Even the smell of the Laboratory brought a sense of excitement to me. I also toyed with the idea of going into Forestry because my love for nature was keen.

I wrote to a dear Aunt Carrie of mine, who lived in Oregon, and shared my seeking dilemma with her. Her reply went something like this:

> "David, life is like a rose. If you try to tear it open you will destroy it, but if you let it unfold, it will become what God intended it to be. "

In effect I heard her saying: Relax and trust. It will become clear to you in its own time.

I enrolled in the College of Science, Literature and Arts, working toward a degree in Psychology, Philosophy and Religion. I enjoyed the campus of the University; I enjoyed the men I was rooming with; I just felt a deep sense of satisfaction with my life at the moment. The GI Bill was sufficient to meet all of my physical needs. What more did I need?

There was at Wesley College a man named Royer Woodburn who was the Director of the Wesley Foundation, a Methodist student fellowship group. LeRoy and I met the Rev. Mr. Woodburn and appreciated him. He got us involved in the Wesley Foundation program. At the same time we signed up for religion courses at Wesley College. There were two instructors: Dr. George Finley who was also manager of a local creamery but taught religion at Wesley, and Dr. George Henry, an older distinguished looking gentleman with white hair who taught religion and philosophy.

Here I was first introduced to a progressive perspective on religion, and a new understanding of the Bible as an inspired work of many persons through centuries of time. The College also had an outstanding music division, organ, piano, voice. Neither of us were involved in any of that.

The fellowship of the Wesley Foundation was just what I needed at that time: a group of friendly, open-minded persons who enjoyed the good life, in a setting of good fellowship and fun. Through Mr. Woodburn's influence I became involved, as well, on the state level of the Methodist Youth Fellowship, and was surprised when I was suddenly elected as the state president of the Methodist Youth Fellowship. This opened all kinds of doors to me – and a spreading circle of friendship, many of whom are still friends today.

In the meantime, Wesley College called a young man to be their new President: Dr. Marcus J. Birrell. Marc had been serving a Methodist Church in the Twin Cities, and in 1948 was chosen to be the President of the little college. He brought a new excitement to the entire scene. He was young and open, warm and outreaching. I was immediately taken into a friendship with him. And when he discovered I could type (what a key!) he hired me to be his Secretary. I served in that capacity until I left the University in the middle of my Senior year. We had such a meaningful relationship; he was a great mentor to me.

In 1957 Marc took a position with a General Board of the Methodist Church in Nashville. In 1959 he was on an out of town speaking engagement and had a heart attack. He died almost immediately. I still miss him!

Somewhat weary of University Dining Hall food a group of us from Wesley Foundation decided to form a cooperative supper club. We hired a cook, and would meet together for our evening meals. This went well, and was also economical. But at Christmas the cook decided to call it quits. What next? In my naivete I said to the group; "If each of you will take turns helping me, I'll cook." And I did! For a group of 20-30 students. It was a great learning and fellowship experience and the experience I gained there has come in handy for me through all stages of my life.

LeRoy and I joined the Tau Kappa Epsilon fraternity, I suppose because we thought it was the thing to do. We went to the Fraternity House for the Monday evening dinner and meeting, and became involved in the social doings of the Fraternity. Most of the men at the time we joined were veterans, and thus quite mature. As younger men joined, the spirit of the Fraternity changed. Drinking increased tremendously. It got so I wouldn't take a girl to a social event anymore as she would have to put up with a group of slobs. So I decided to withdraw from the Fraternity, along with a couple of other fellows who had become discouraged by the excessive drinking also.

I then became involved in the Independent Student group, and was eventually nominated by them for President of our Senior Class. I did some campaigning but not much. As a result I lost to the Greek candidate by 2 votes! I must admit I was relieved.

My involvement in the religion classes at Wesley College was fascinating. I remember the words of my home town pastor before I left for the University: "David, if you go to the University you will lose your religion." My reply: "Louie, if it makes me lose my religion then it isn't worth having."
Contrary to my local Pastor's judgment it was here I began to

experience a meaningful personal faith. In the courses at Wesley College I was exposed to positive images of a Progressive Religion that set me on a searching course for the rest of my ministry. It wasn't a shock when I arrived at Seminary to be exposed to like-minded ideas.

I was elected President of the Wesley Foundation and this gave me a relationship freedom that I had not experienced before. I began to go out to local churches on "deputation teams" to tell about Wesley College and the Wesley Foundation program. I began to feel comfortable behind a pulpit.
I met a lot of the leadership of the church and I began to feel my interests beginning to move toward a religious vocation.

My first chance to vote was in the Presidential election of 1948. I went to the voting site to vote. The attendant told me that I couldn't vote because I was not a resident of Grand Forks. I had quite an argument with her before she finally allowed me to vote. Eventually I convinced her that since I had spent over two years in the Navy, and now two years at the University, this was essentially my home. Had I told her who I was going to vote for she probably wouldn't have allowed it. I voted for Norman Thomas who was the Socialist candidate for that election, and for several elections afterward for that matter. It's interesting to look back to discover how much of what Norman Thomas advocated has now become a part of our on-going society. Thomas was a great mind and a great spirit.

I never shared with my parents whom I had voted for. My Dad was a solid Republican. He always made it clear that he was a "Lincoln Republican." As a youngster of course I followed my father's line of thinking.   Most of the children in my class apparently were Democrats because I had several wrestling matches to prove the superiority of the Republican candidate. The one memory that is particularly vivid to me was the year

1936 when Alf Landon was the Republican candidate, a man from Kansas. His icon was the sunflower, and when I first went to school wearing a large Alf Landon sunflower the feuds began.

The Beginning of a Long Journey

"Love all of God's creation, the whole and every grain of sand in it. Love every leaf, every ray of God's light. Love the animals, love the plants, love everything. If you love everything you will perceive the Divine nature in things. Once you perceive it you will begin to comprehend it every day and you will come at last to love the whole world with an all-embracing love." – Dostoyevsky, The Brothers Karamazov

My cousin John Knecht and his wife Lorraine were very involved in a young adult fellowship group at First United Methodist Church in Fargo. I was very involved in the Wesley Foundation at the University. Once or twice a year our groups would meet together at one site or the other. On a trip through Fargo I stopped at the A.C. (North Dakota State Agricultural College) to visit John and Lorraine. As we visited they mentioned that there was an attractive brown haired, brown eyed girl in their group that I ought to meet. The idea was at least implanted in my mind although I wasn't to meet her yet for some time.

Jane Sheldon had completed two years of college at the A.C. Times right then were tough for her parents to provide further education. Jane persuaded them to at least support a summer experience in a Methodist Caravan, which was a program in which college age students would work in local churches to help with their youth program. Jane made the trip to California to serve as a Caravan representative, which turned out to be a determinative influence on her future life.

When she came back to her home near Wheatland, ND in late August, her parents showed her a small news clip they had taken from the Fargo Forum. It was an ad for the school at Wimbledon urgently needing a 5th and 6th grade teacher. This was the week-end before school was to start on Monday. Her father took her to Wimbledon to meet with the Board.

Jane's father, Charles Sheldon, drove her to Wimbledon to meet with some of the School Board to make application for the job. She met two women, Mrs. Ralph Trangsrude and Mrs. Peggy Rose. (Incidentally, Mrs. Trangsrude had been my teacher in the 3rd and 4th grades. She was one of my favorite teachers.)

The two women indicated that they were to drive out to a field where Mr. Patterson was combining. He would join them and carry out the interview. As they drive into the country they carried on a conversation of small talk. When they arrived at the field where Mr. Patterson was combining, he recognized their car, shut down his machinery, and came ambling over to meet them. They opened the window to talk with him. One of them introduced "Miss Sheldon" who would like to apply for the position of 5th and 6th grade teacher. She told them of her educational qualifications and that she would be teaching for the year under an emergency certificate until she completed the educational requirements. A few questions and answers were exchanged.

Then one of the women put this question to her: "Do you run around much?" Jane's reply: "Not too much." Then came a round of exchange between the three Board members: "Well what do you think, Morris?" "I hired the last one; what do you think?" and the sparring went on for a while until at least they declared she was hired. Then one of the women added: "We have a saying around here that if you don't get a husband in two years you might as well move on."

This was an interesting experience that only she can share with all of the nuances of the experience. The Board did hire her, and she moved to Wimbledon and started teaching on Monday, with an "emergency certificate" since she had taken no education courses in College to that date.

Neither of us were aware, of course, at this point, that the comment of one of the Board would prove true: she would catch a husband within the two years!

My Dad used to tell the story of her first visit to the Methodist Church at Wimbledon. Apparently the church was quite full, and Miss Sheldon had to walk down the aisle to a pew near the front. Her hat had a bouncing feather that jiggled as she walked by. He always reminded her of that.

I have mentioned before how my parents' home was an "open house" to anyone, but especially to single teachers who were expected to stay in town on weekends. On one of these weekends I came home to visit the folks, and there was Miss Sheldon – the brown haired, brown eyed woman that my cousins had referred to. I was interested. More interesting perhaps is that she had seen a picture on the desk of me in my Navy uniform. She wrote back to her parents: "I just met the man I am going to marry, but he doesn't know it yet."

In the Spring of 1949 Dr. Henry Gernhardt, who was Pastor of Epworth Methodist Church in Valley City, had a heart attack. Out of the blue the Cabinet of the ND Conference of the Methodist Church approached me asking if I would consider filling in the pulpit of the Valley City church for the summer. After careful consideration I agreed, and I moved into the old parsonage in Valley City.

I did preach through the summer, but perhaps the most meaningful part of the summer to me and to the congregation was the work I did with the youth. We had a couple of lads who were going through some rough places in their lives at that time and I was ready to listen – and that was meaningful to them.

It just so happened that Miss Jane Sheldon had enrolled at Valley City State Teachers College for the summer. She showed up at church on one of my first Sundays, and I was delighted. I asked her if she would be willing to work with me with the youth for the summer. She agreed. Our first activity was to be a picnic with the Junior High Youth. We ended up with one boy, one girl, and Miss Sheldon and I! We still had a fun picnic. But this opened the door for invitations to Miss Sheldon to have coffee occasionally, so we got to know each other quite well.

As Fall arrived I moved back to the dormitory in Grand Forks for my Senior year at the University. By this time I had firmed up my Call to Ministry. A lot of factors entered into that, not least of which was my experience as the President of the Wesley Foundation, my experiences on Deputation teams, and my relationship to Dr. Marcus Birrell and the Rev. Royer Woodburn. This was the Fall I ALMOST made it to being President of the senior Class. As it turned out it was good I lost the election.

Sometime in late Fall the Pastor of the Federated Church at Lisbon left for another appointment, and again the Cabinet came to ask if I would consider filling out the appointment until a new Pastor could be assigned in June.

I was enjoying my Senior year. It would mean giving up a lot of meaningful relationships for an experience I couldn't even imagine. It would mean completing at least two courses by correspondence, which I did not look forward to. Overall I decided to give it a try.

Essentially there was no public transportation to Lisbon, which was located about 140 miles south of Grand Forks, so it was necessary for me to move there. A bedroom was available for me at the Manse; the lower level was rented out temporarily. I could fix simple meals there, but most of the time I went down the street a couple of blocks to The Coffee Cup Cafe – a dining counter affair that was run by a divorcee named Leona Gamache. Her husband had walked out on her and left her to raise a family of five boys. Two of them were old enough to give her some help in the
Café, so I met them.

As I got to know the family and enjoyed the relationship , Leona kind of "adopted" me as a member of her family, and I enjoyed the family. The third boy, Gene, was a top notch basketball player, and eventually went to the Agricultural College and was a varsity player there. Gene and I got to be good friends. Occasionally I would loan him my car for a date. Our paths since then have gone very different directions, but we still keep in touch with each other.

The drag for me in the midst of the early Spring was keeping up with the correspondence courses. My heart wasn't with them and my reluctance to work on them lowered my 4.0 average a bit, but I still graduated with High Honors. I had achieved the Phi Beta Kappa recognition earlier.

The Lisbon congregation was a Federated Church – a union of the Presbyterian Church and the Methodist Church. The "marriage" was not particularly congenial. Differences became emphasized every Fall because they would worship in one of the church buildings one year and then change to the other building the next year. Pastors who were assigned were also chosen alternately: Methodist/Presbyterian.

The joy of the summer was once again the youth group. It became quite a group as the summer developed. I think in all we had over twenty youth. I held a confirmation class for those who wished to join the church. There were 15 of them, most of them from the Presbyterian side of the Federation. None of the local people gave me any warnings, but after I had officially received them into the church I had a visit from the Presbyterian conference minister, and he blistered my ears. I had no business confirming these youth without first presenting them to the local Presbytery, and then to him for final approval. This was probably my first experience with the "officialdom" of the church. I rather think God enjoyed it all!

Another outstanding event of the summer: I purchased my first new automobile – a 1950 Studebaker Champion. One of the members of the congregation was in the automobile business and thanks to his assistance I was able to work out the details to make it possible. It was a dark blue Studebaker Champion, and the cost of it at that time was $ 1,871. I was granted a little over $500 for my old Chevrolet that I traded in. That little Studebaker was a great little automobile, and it took care of our needs through the three years I was in seminary, and on into our first parish.

My decision to enter the ministry led to the next necessary decision: where to go to Seminary. I chose the Labor Day week-end to make a trip back east to visit some possible seminaries. I knew of Boston School of Theology, so I went there first to investigate. It so happened they were just moving into their new building, so they had no time to spend on a peon from afar.

I had read some things by faculty members at Union Seminary in New York City, NY and was favorably impressed. I journeyed up there, only to discover they were closed for the weekend. I came back to the campus of Yale Divinity School, to discover that they also were closed. Having no place to stay I spent a cold, wet night on the "porch" of the Yale Chapel, with the hope that someone might come by and take pity on me. No one did.

My next stop on the way home was Garrett Biblical Institute in Evanston, IL. I was afraid that it too might be closed, but there was one student staying over in the dorm.   He was a young man from Minnesota. He had just completed his second year of seminary. He arranged for some bedding, and I stayed with him in his dormitory room. It was a fortuitous experience! It gave me a chance to talk with a student about his experience, his overview of the faculty, his sense of the spirit of the place. And when I left there the next day my mind was made up. I would go to Garrett Biblical Institute in Evanston.

Arrangements had to be made in a hurry for registration, finances, residence, etc. Fortunately I still had GI Bill to go on for expenses. Everything fell into place and I steered my little Champion Studebaker back east to Evanston, Illinois.

 I was assigned to a dormitory room on the east end of the east dormitory building. As I looked out my window I was greeted by Lake Michigan. Since then Northwestern University has built out into the Lake by dredging sand in by the millions of tons, so one can no longer see the Lake from Garrett. I came to love the lake like a person. Some days it would greet me with a bright, sunny disposition that established my mood for the day. Other days it was angry and foreboding, and its "relationship" had to be dealt with in my own soul.

The spirit of the student body was excellent: international, ecumenical, open-minded. As I look back on it, it was the right place to be. I made several lasting friendships there. My memories are gilded. Through these weeks of 1950-51 the US Postal Service kept the relationship between Jane Sheldon and myself growing more deeply, so much that we began to plan for a summer of '51 wedding. She began to investigate possibilities for employment as a teacher somewhere near Evanston.

Meanwhile, back in North Dakota. Once more the Conference of the Methodist Church placed a heavy hand on my shoulder. Would I be willing to supply the Church at Harvey, ND for the summer. As I recall I spent three to four days of the week at Harvey. I roomed with a railroad family whose name I cannot remember! They were kind to me. I served both the Harvey congregation and a congregation at Goodrich, about thirty miles away.

Basically the summer was uneventful at Harvey. Jane and my relationship matured, and we planned an August wedding. In those days a blood test was necessary to get a marriage license. Jane came up to Harvey with me one weekend, and we arranged with Dr. Beck, a medical doctor and a member of the Harvey congregation, to take our blood between the Church Service at Harvey and the one at Goodrich. It worked!

Jane and her mother began planning for the wedding. It was to be in the little Wheatland Church on August 12. We would ask friend Marc Birrell to "tie the knot." The Sheldon family was quite extensive so the planning expanded, but it was fun.

Jane had an Uncle Wayne who was a prankster. The church had one of the old furnace registers in the floor under the place we were to stand during the wedding. Wayne threatened to roll a dime down the floor to let it drop down the register during the ring ceremony. As the time for the ring ceremony approached I was uptight, because Wayne was capable of doing something like that – but he didn't.

Poor Mother Sheldon was quite nervous about the wedding. She was highly sedated the day of the wedding so I'm not sure she was completely cognizant of what was happening until it was all over. But all the details were taken care of.

Some of Jane's cousins mischievously smeared the engine block of our little Studebaker with Limburger Cheese. That created quite an aroma as we headed to Fargo to spend our wedding night at the Gladstone Hotel. Wedding nights are wedding nights, whoever or wherever you may be. Agreements to forego intimacy on that first night are melted away by the sight of one's beloved in whatever circumstances.

The Al Geisler family from the Valley City church was kind enough to loan us their cabin on Lake Pelican for our Honeymoon getaway. It was homey and quiet, and the days were good. Circumstances sometimes have a way of revealing unknown details until pressed to reveal themselves. I had assumed through all the time of our courtship that a young woman brought up on a North Dakota farm would know all that would be necessary to put a decent meal on the table. Wrong! As we were going to be honeymooning in a cabin where meals had to be prepared, the very act of buying groceries before making our way to the cabin revealed that Jane had not done that kind of thing before. So my brief experience cooking for a group of students in a cooperative supper club at UND proved to be a gift, and I became the chief cook of our time at the cabin, and until Jane had time to learn for herself from the Betty Crocker cookbook that she had spirited away from the Wedding Gift Table.

We had time to make one more quick trip to visit each of our parents before taking off for Evanston again in OUR little Studebaker – now as man and wife. After weeks of negotiation during the summer Jane was granted a contract to teach Sixth Grade at Harper School in Wilmette, IL. With her salary, the remnants of my GI Bill, and part time work by me our future seemed secure.

We landed in Evanston, and at the invitation of friends who were already established there, we had a bed to sleep on, and an apartment to retreat to, until we were able to find our own housing. We will be ever grateful to Ron and Faye for their hospitality. Ron and I had been roommates in the dormitory for our first year at the Seminary.

After some searching for an apartment within our budget we came upon 1234 Chicago Avenue. This was a large old house, built sometime at the end of the 19th century.

The landlady was as strange her house, but we came to appreciate her in the year we lived there. She lived on the first floor, a Garrett couple lived on the second floor, and we climbed the steps to the third floor. The apartment was at the back of the house which abutted the El tracks (elevated train) that extended to most of the communities up the North Shore The trains rumbled by on regular schedule day and night, and we soon learned that conversation could only take place at the interstices of silence after the trains rumbled by.

The apartment had one large room, which became our living room, dining room, and bedroom. The ceilings sloped down on either side so the only place one could walk upright was in the center of the room. At one end of that room a doorway led into a narrow hallway, perhaps eight feet long. Immediately inside the hallway was our kitchen, with a small gas counter-top range, and a small refrigerator. Going on through the hallway one came to the bathroom which was our source of water, and the place where dishwashing could be done. It was not much to look at, but it was our very first home. It provided for all the needs we had for our first year together.

The roughest part of that first year was Jane's teaching job. The School System in Wilmette was just emerging from "progressive education," an experiment which allowed the students to do whatever they chose to do as long as they didn't hang from the chandeliers. It was a difficult year for Jane, and for me, as sometimes she would come home from school weeping over the trials of the day. Thankfully her second year at Wilmette was a real joy, thanks to the preparations made by their teacher the year before.

For the first few weeks I found employment at the Washington National Insurance company at $1.10 an hour. My job was to close out cancelled insurance policies – a most boring job. But the people with whom I worked were an interesting mix of souls who were "doing what they could."

I next found a job with National School of Education, driving a school bus. The "bus" was really a large station wagon with benches along each side of the rear of the wagon. It is difficult for me to believe now, but we had about twenty youngsters in that "suicide vehicle."   I had two youngsters in the front seat with me. My first day was hell on wheels. The student sitting next to me was a tiny child, perhaps a third grader. At one point he said, "I liked Big Jim (their former driver). He made us behave!" So my German blood kicked in.

The next morning when we started out to school all pandemonium broke loose. I immediately pulled to the side of the street, stopped the bus, and declared: 'Boys and Girls, I have all day. We will sit here until you sit down and behave as you know you should." That took care of the situation. They knew I meant what I said and I don't believe I had to demonstrate it again.

Chicago was an exciting city. We had time to see the Aquarium, The Art Museum, and the Field Museum and some other sights of that great city. The courses at the Seminary were stimulating. We had many opportunities to get to know students and spouses from across the country and overseas. The warmth of the fellowship became a healing and encouraging spirit in which to live that first year together.

A Pastor in the United Methodist Church never becomes a member of a local church. He/she is a member of the Annual Conference, which is a body of lay and clergy responsible for the administration of the congregations within its jurisdiction, called The Annual Conference. The annual gathering of the Conference in the North Dakota was usually about the first week of June. We made arrangements for the journey back to attend the North Dakota Annual Conference.

With the break in the school in June we said goodbye to 1234 Chicago Avenue, and found another apartment a few blocks away at 928 Elmwood Avenue. This apartment gave us two rooms – we enjoyed the extra space, and the fact that our daytime lives could be separated from our bedroom. The handicap was that we shared a bathroom with another Garrett couple who lived on the next floor up, and a little old lady who lived across the hall. With a little adjustment the arrangement worked out perfectly.

I decided to attend summer classes, and Jane came along to audit the classes. We spent several week-ends with a couple from Pennsylvania, Barbara and Reed Hurst. Reed was serving a small church in rural Illinois. After summer school we drove back to Dakota and divided the month before school began between our families. The days went fast, and it was soon time to return to Evanston for our last year of Seminary. It was actually good to see 928 Elmwood again.

Jane went back to Harper School for another year. This year was a joy. Her friend, Babette Fleming, had taught the class the year before when they were fifth graders. Babette was an excellent teacher so they had a good foundation.

The children in Harper School, for the most part, came from prominent homes. Jane had students from the Florsheim family, and the Kraft family, for example. We were invited out to dinner at the home of one of her students. On the menu was roast beef. As the master of the house began carving the roast one could almost hear the cow 'MOO," the roast was so rare. This was our first experience with really RARE roast beef. I must admit it took some getting used to.

When we returned to Evanston I was able to find another part time job. This time I was stock boy for the Notions Department of the Evanston Marshall Field Store. This job was to put me in touch with those who lived near the peak of the economic pyramid. These people bought their supplies by the case: Kleenex, Tampax, Toilet Paper, Paper Towels.

The experience also put me in touch with an experience in human nature that was new to me. Perhaps I had just been naïve! A woman named Nora was in charge of the Notions Department She was a wonderful person to know, and an excellent administrator. She had to be.

The Department staff consisted of six female clerks.   One of them was off each day. When that woman was gone the rest of the staff "feasted " on her as though she was carrion. Nora (the Department Head) and I used to find amusing the way they could talk about that woman in such negative terms when they must have each realized that on their own day off they would be the "feast." It is so strange to me that we human beings seem to have a hard time growing beyond the place where someone else's foibles become a part of our plot to build ourselves up. Could we but accept ourselves for who we are, and others for whom they are, what a great world this would be.

Our last year of Seminary seemed to go so fast. Sometime in March Jane surprised me with the exciting news that she was pregnant. This increased our yearning for our schools to be completed so we could return to the Dakotas, be assigned to a parish, and get on with life. But our first job now was to begin a relationship with an OBGYN.

As June approached we made plans for our trip home. When Jane shared with her Doctor that we were making a quick driving trip home to attend Annual Conference he put the brakes on. Our solution was finally that Jane would go to Fargo by train in time for my Ordination at First United Methodist Church on June 14. I would drive in our trusty little Studebaker. Then Jane would return to Evanston by train while my parents and I drove back to Evanston. This put us back to Evanston in time for my graduation from Seminary, and my parents could be there for the occasion.

Dr. Horace Greeley Smith was President of the Seminary at that time. He had taught at GBI for years, and then was elected President. He was going to retire this year. Sometime before graduation he called me to his office. "David," he said, "you have had a splendid record here at Garrett. We are grateful for you, and the Seminary would like to offer you the opportunity to continue your studies here on a fellowship." That's a paraphrase of his actual words, but that was the weight of it. What an honor! But my response was something like this: "Dr. Smith, I am grateful for the generosity of your offer – and perhaps the day may come when I will choose to go that path, but right now I am anxious to return to the Dakotas and have a parish of my own." Before our conversation ended he gave me the opportunity to look over his extensive library and choose any book that I wished. I still have it in my library: THE CHARACTER OF JESUS by Charles Edward Jefferson. It is long out of print, but I have discovered recently that it has been re-published.

Pageantry and Profession

"The Miracles of the Church seem to me to rest not so much upon forces or voices or healing power suddenly coming near to us from afar off, but upon our perceptions being made finer, that for a moment our eyes can see and our ears can hear what is all about us always." – Willa Cather, Death Comes to the Archbishop

It was a great feeling to march in the Graduation Procession at the end of my time at Garrett, with the cord over my shoulders indicating I had graduated with honors. It was also a great feeling to pack up our limited possessions, and to drive back home to North Dakota with my parents. Jane came along by train and we met her in Fargo.

The Annual Conference was an especially exciting affair knowing that at the conclusion of the Conference there would be the reading of appointments which would indicate where we would be living in our first parish. An interesting sidelight: when we were home at Christmas the talk of the Cabinet was that we would probably be assigned to the Lidgerwood parish, so on our drive back to Seminary after Christmas we drove through Lidgerwood to see what the community and church looked like.

Continuing our journey back to Evanston we drove through the little community of Fairmount nearby. We found the church, a beautiful, fairly new little structure. Alongside of it was a large, dark green square house. We speculated that it may be the Parsonage. Wouldn't it be fun to live here?

By the time the appointments were read at Annual Conference, it had been decided by the Cabinet that we would be assigned to the Fairmount-Bethany Charge. Hurray!

On June 14 I was ordained as an Elder of the Methodist Church. Bishop Edwin Voigt was our presiding Bishop – a Prince of a man. When we were settled in our Parsonage at Fairmount we invited Bishop Voigt to come for a week-end with us. He and his wife came, and were such a delight. An unforgettable experience was watching Bishop Voigt help Jane wipe breakfast dishes in our old kitchen.

We arrived in Fairmount on June 28, 1953. The Parsonage was the large, square, green house about which we had fantasized. We had scrounged a few pieces of furniture from our parents' homes. We made a trip to nearby Wahpeton, and visited Vertin's Furniture where we purchased a dining room set, a davenport and chair, and a bedroom set. Then there was the matter of furnishing the nursery for our first child's birth in December.

On our first Sunday there we had to stop at a farmhouse to be sure of our way to the little Bethany Church out in the country, and it happened to be a family that was getting ready to go to Bethany for our first service there.

Before we began the service at Fairmount a stately looking woman came to me and introduced herself. "I want you to know Pastor that if the noon siren blows before you are done I will get up and leave." I appreciate frank people, and I came to appreciate this dear soul many times, because one never had to wonder what she was thinking. Jane had an experience with her at a Study Club as well. They were discussing health insurance. Jane said, "We almost make money on our child birth experiences." Our first three children were 1 ½ years apart. This woman responded: " I wondered why you were having your children so close together." Refreshing!

We spent the summer getting acquainted with our parish families, going to summer camps, canning vegetables from a large garden that old Charlie had planted in anticipation of our coming. It seemed we were on a "high" at every move. I purchased an old oak desk from the local Doctor for $25.00. I purchased lumber from the local lumberyard and built shelves in one of the rooms on the ground floor that became my Study.

Imagine my surprise when I went to the local lumber yard to buy the boards to discover that the Manager was none other than our lumberyard man, and Community Band leader in Wimbledon – Art Lindahl. He became a great friend. Along with this surprise was the realization that it was Art's wife who had tried to give piano lessons to a six old boy almost 20 years before! She still wore heavy perfume!

As winter approached we realized that the big old house could get cold. We also discovered we had mice: basement, first floor, upstairs. One of our next acquisitions was a beautiful little orange farm cat who gave us no end of pleasure as she ran from one end of the lower level to the other, ultimately jumping up on the back of a rocking chair and enjoying the ride until the rocking stopped. She also helped solve the mouse problem

Across the street from us was a Mobil gas station run by a young man, Dick Wilson. Together with the asset of having service so close at hand, Dick and I became good friends. His station was a place for several of the old men of the village to gather and "gossip." In October Dick knew I was to go to Nashville, TN for a youth worker's conference. Somewhere along the line he must have indicated this was to take place.

That Jane was very pregnant with our first child was evident to everyone. When these old men put together the fact that I was going to go to Nashville for a week, and that my wife was "very" pregnant, they let their concerns be known. And Richard was to let me know what they thought about it. I assured Dick that Jane's Doctor had put his O.K. on the plan, and I went to Nashville as planned.

In those years singing groups from Rust College, a black college in Holly Springs, MS, would make pilgrimages through the upper Midwest to acquaint us with their needs, and also to entertain us with some of the finest choral singing I have ever heard. At that time their Director was a lovely woman named Natalie Doxey. I became acquainted with her as a child because when the troupe came to Wimbledon Miss Doxey would always stay at our house.

When they came to Fairmount Miss Doxey was staying with us. The singers were staying with other families of the Church.

On December 3 it became evident to Jane and I that it was time for her to go to Breckenridge, MN, where our hospital was, as it was likely our first child would be born that night. Miss Doxey was insistent that she should go along with us so she could "hold Jane's hand." We finally convinced her to stay and take care of the house, and any calls that might come in.

Our first child, Kathleen Louise, was born at 7:57 a.m. the next morning. I had come home late at night. Miss Doxey was still up at midnight. I finally convinced her to get some sleep, and I tried to get some sleep as well. During the night a baby blizzard came up with howling winds and drifting snow. When I received the called that Kathleen had been born I roused two or three of the Rust College Singers (male type) to accompany me. The roads were drivable, but there were periodic finger drifts across the highway that would make the car shudder when we hit them. None of these boys had even seen snow before, let alone snow drifts on a highway. It was entertaining to me to see them grip the sides of the car as we hit a finger drift along the way. But our journey was safe, and looking back on the experience from the safety of our living room they admitted they had enjoyed the experience, and could laugh about it.

The Fairmount-Bethany Charge was struggling to some degree. They had a couple of difficult situations with Pastors, and the churches had felt that impact. Fairmount hadn't been able to pay its Conference obligations for a few years. Bethany didn't have that problem because its Treasurer was a bachelor who was financially sound, and a very generous person, and when the Treasury needed money he would take care of the obligation himself.

Apparently the arrival of a young parish pastor ("you look like a high school kid") and his wife was a refreshing breath of air. The feeling was mutual. I was so exhilarated by the experience that I was on a high – most of the time.

Of course there were other times.

In those years the Methodist Church was very involved in settling refugees from the aftermath of World War II. At one Official Board meeting I presented to them a proposal to sponsor a refugee family. The family consisted of a man, his wife, and two children. Our responsibility was to provide housing and find work for the husband to do. We would also have responsibility for transportation costs to Fairmount. Of course the Board wanted to know more about the family. "Well, Joe was a prisoner of war in America during the war, stationed in a POW camp at Bismarck." "Were they members of a church?" "Yes, they were of Catholic background." "What were the ages of the children? Does the husband have any skills?" It went on for a few minutes. The Chairman raised the question of whether we should sponsor or not. A vote was taken. The answer was unanimously "NO." I felt the blood rush to my head. My old German anger kicked. One of the men on the Board was a prominent member of the American Legion. At this time the American Legion was engaged in a campaign to place the words "this nation UNDER God" in our pledge of allegiance. So, as my anger exploded I said as calmly as I could: "It's interesting how much we are struggling right now to place the words "under God" in our Pledge of Allegiance to the flag. And here is an opportunity to reach out in God's Name to give a hand to a needy family in the Name of that God." And I was quiet. You could have heard a pin drop. Then a dear soul from the Board, a single woman who served so capably in so many areas of the work of the congregation, said very quietly: "I move we reconsider." One could feel the movement of the Spirit in that place. A vote was taken and the result was a unanimous decision to undertake the project.

The next morning I had an anonymous letter in the mail, a small piece of paper on which was printed simply these words from Scripture: "In patience possess ye your soul." I was sure I knew the source: two devoted folk who loved the church – and also loved me. The remembrance of this has been a guard and stay for me many times when tempted to strike out in impatience and anger.

This venture with the refugee family turned out to be a wonderful experience for everyone. The congregation found a vacant house to rent. They gathered furniture, clothing and household utensils They rented a freeze box at the local Locker Plant and filled it with food, and they had a shower to gather beginning food for the family. It was discovered that Joe had been an expert mechanic, and he was hired by a local auto repair shop, and proved himself a wonderful asset. To add to all of this, the congregation paid its Conference apportionments in full. The Fishers remained in Fairmount for several years. When Joe died the family moved to Wahpeton. What a tremendous experience it was.

We had a super youth group. Youth seemed to come out of the woodwork. Part of it, I am sure, is that we were young. The old Lutheran Pastor was a dour soul who wouldn't even say good morning to me when I met him on the sidewalk as I went to get the mail. The Catholic Priest was an old man, who had soured of life in his later years. The youth were alive, and active, and did some amazing projects during the four years we were there, and beyond.

We had some interesting people in that congregation, as there are in all congregations: There was Charlie who insisted on hoeing our garden, although I assured him over and over again that I enjoyed gardening. He would sometimes come to the door of the Parsonage while the children were taking their naps. Our front door had a chime doorbell which with one tap would sound: "Bing bong." Charley insisted on pressing it several times: "bing bong, bing bong, bing bong, bing bong."

There was a woman of the community who came to every funeral, even though she didn't know the family. "I want to show them my support." I remember one funeral where she came in the last minute with her hair tied up in curlers: "Whose funeral is this?"

There was the little woman, with roving eyes, who loved to share the last bit of gossip she had heard, with the admonition, "Don't tell anyone now."

But there were so many down-to-earth people, with a simple, straight-forward Faith, who loved God, who loved the church, who loved other people, and who loved us, even in our sometimes fumbling ministry. Years later we were asked which was the best congregation we had served. The answer always is, "We enjoyed them all." But Fairmount and Bethany would certainly be at the top of the list with the others.

Two more of our daughters were born while we were at Fairmount: Margaret on August 10, 1955 – Easter Sunday. We had taken Jane to Breckenridge the night before as she felt the time was near. I came home for the night as nothing was happening. We had an Easter Sunrise Service early on Sunday morning. A check with Jane after the service indicated that Margaret had been born, so I had the regular services and then went to Breckenridge to welcome our second daughter – a tiny babe with a mop of dark hair.

Jeanne was born about a year and a half later – August 17. There were no dramatic situations about her birth as far as the daily schedule was concerned, but of course it was exciting to welcome into our family a third little daughter.

Death visited our family for the first time since our marriage. Grandpa Sheldon died on November 23. On the 24th my father had a slight heart attack that put him to bed. My Mother took over the management of the store and the bottle gas business. The bottle gas business involved filling the cylinders when necessary, and Dad had built a platform for this purpose on our garage building at the house. The cylinders were filled from the delivery truck. As she was filling a bottle, apparently the static caused by her silk slip ignited a fire. Fortunately the truck could be backed away from the fire but the building was a complete loss. Thanks to the Wimbledon Volunteer Fire department there was no injury to Mother, nor did the fire threaten the home which was nearby.

I was named by the Annual Conference to serve as the Conference Youth Director. The responsibility was to oversee the work of the Methodist Youth Fellowship across the state: youth convocations, spiritual life retreats, sub-district activities. I received some training for the job at national headquarters in Nashville, TN. I served in this capacity for nine years until my responsibilities in the parish made it seem necessary to pass the job on to someone else. Besides I wasn't getting any younger.

Another death in the family: Grandma Sheldon in Wheatland. By this time it seems I had become the unofficial "chaplain" of the Sheldon family: deaths, marriages, baptisms.

Also during this year Dad Knecht had another heart attack that was to slow him down considerably.

Pulling up Roots

"The story of a saint is always a love story. It is a story of a God who loves, and of the beloved who learns how to reciprocate ad share that 'harsh and dreadful '. It is a story that includes misunderstanding, deception, betrayal, concealment, reversal, and revelation of character. It is, if the saints are to be trusted, our story. But to be a saint is not to be a solitary lover. It is to enter into deeper community with everyone and everything that exists."
  – Kenneth L. Woodward, Making Saints

We were finishing up our fourth year in the parish of Fairmount and Bethany. At the end of each year there is a Charge Conference in the Methodist Church where reports of the year are summarized, and a motion is made either to have the Pastor returned, or for the Cabinet to consider a move. That moment came at this Charge Conference. We were meeting in the little Bethany Church. A large, prominent member of the congregation got to his feet: "Mr. Gernhardt, (our District Superintendent) I was talking to a man on the faculty of the college this last week and he said to me, 'We're going to get your Pastor'. I said to him, "The hell you are!" But I want to know, Mr. Gernhardt, if there is any truth to that." Dr. Gernhardt was a master "manipulator," and he ducked the question completely. But there was a pall over the meeting from that moment on.

At Annual Conference in June we were assigned to Faith Methodist Church in Fargo. It was a congregation that came out of old First Methodist Church down town. On Easter Sunday, April 10, 1955, several of the congregation marched the 20 blocks to the site of the new congregation. They had purchased the old building once used by the American

Lutheran Church on 12th Avenue and 10th Street and had it moved to the new site on the corner of N. Tenth Street and 19th Avenue. The first Pastor assigned was Dr. A. B. Smith, a former District Superintendent. Dr. Smith served the parish one year, and 5 months, and died suddenly of a heart attack. In the interim the congregation was served by the ministry of First Church, until our arrival in June of 1957.

On the evening before our first Sunday we had been invited out to my boyhood church in Wimbledon to speak at a Father-Son Banquet. Since my parents still lived there our entire family went along. When we came out of the church at the conclusion of the banquet someone met us at the door announcing that a tornado had struck the city of Fargo and the whole north side of the city had been wiped out. The "north side" is where our Parsonage was, and where the church was. We tried to make a phone call to someone to get details, but there were no phone calls allowed to anyone we knew. In talking with the Police Department, I identified myself, and they told me I couldn't get into town until the next morning, and that would have to be with some identification.

As you can imagine it was a sleepless night for me. I drove to Fargo first thing in the morning, and was able to make contact with two men of the congregation. They met me and escorted me into town. Fortunately the whole "north side" of Fargo had not been wiped out, but there was a lot of damage, and several people had been killed and many injured.

Through the next few days, with the help of these men from the congregation, I was able to make contact with every family of the congregation. Some had suffered property damage. One family had been struck on their way home from a picnic at Oakgrove Park. They had not been as fortunate. The daughter, a girl of 5 or 6 was uninjured and was rescued by someone who saw her wandering around in a daze. A small son, only months old , ended up in one of the hospitals. The father was taken to the Veterans Hospital, and the Mother was taken to still another hospital. We were finally able to make contact with all, to assure the parents that everyone was alive and that their daughter was being cared for by friends.

Our little church building was somewhat battered by debris and hail. The experience bound the new congregation together in a powerful way.

The Faith Congregation was made up mainly of young families with young children. None of them were financially well-fixed, but they had great spirit, and picked up life where it had been interrupted.

The congregation had temporarily rented a small house on 21st Avenue North for the Parsonage. That became our home. It was small for our family of five, but comfortable. There was only a slab where the garage was to be built. The family will not let me forget that one time coming home, I drove up on the slab, and seeing the neighbor's wife in their back yard ahead (she did have beautiful legs!) I drove off the slab. Embarrassing.

There were a lot of children and youth in the congregation. We had a super youth group again. We still keep contact with some of them. It was exciting to be Pastor of a new congregation and to help them as they chose the direction for their future. One of the first projects was the building of a Parsonage on a lot close to the church. The project was planned and completed with such a congenial spirit it was a joy to behold. The neighborhood provided friendly neighbors, and many children for our children to play with.

Across 19th Avenue from the church was the old Fair Grounds – a wide open territory from Broadway west to University Drive, and from 19th Avenue North to 17th Avenue North. In the Fall the annual County Fair brought a gathering of people and livestock of all sizes shapes and descriptions. And with all of the barns filled with livestock we inherited a horde of flies while the Fair was being held and for a while afterwards. But we survived. At that time the little frame church building stood basically by itself on the north side of the city.

As time went on, planning began for the building of the Sanctuary unit of the new church building.

This unit of our planned development was completed in 1963, and dedicated on the Sunday following the assassination of President Kennedy. An occasion that should have been one of great exaltation was muted by the grief for our young President.

To the west of the church, not far away, was Hector Airport. There was a lot of pressure to develop the land up to the airport with commercial buildings. The city mayor at that time, was Herschel Lashkowitz. He was a farsighted man, and feared that to surround the airport with commercial development would lead to pressure to move the airport farther out from the city. He wanted to enlist me, as a Pastor close to the area, to help alert the citizenry of the danger so the city fathers would take action to keep that from happening.

On this particular evening I was down at the old Central High School with a group of youth on a swimming party. We were just leaving the pool to go home, and I was in the dressing room drying off to get dressed. The custodian came into the dressing room and announced: "Pastor, the Mayor is in the hallway and he urgently wants to talk with you." Just then the

Mayor pushed his way into the dressing room. There I sat bare naked on the bench wiping my feet so I could get dressed, and he began a long speech of appeal. When I finally could get a word in I suggested that it would be helpful if I could get dressed, so we could get the youth back to the church where their parents were coming to pick them up. I was finally able to convince him to get together the next morning, and we would talk about what could be done. As you can imagine the boys in the dressing room had quite a laugh over that one.

One of the couples who belonged to Faith Church was Wally Johnson and his wife. Wally was an officer with the North Dakota Air National Guard with headquarters at Hector Field in Fargo. A Lutheran Pastor, Lloyd Zaudtke, had been serving as a volunteer Chaplain for the unit but he did not want to continue. Wally asked me if I would consider joining the Air National Guard as its Chaplain. After Jane and I had considered what it might mean for the future, and after I had discussed it with members of the Administrative Board of the Church, I began the process of enlisting.

I first had to be approved by the Methodist Church. Necessary contacts were made and permission was given. This was no problem. Then I had to be approved by the Pentagon. This entailed a trip to Washington, D.C. to meet with the Chaplain Department at the Pentagon. The local Air Guard unit arranged for me to ride down to Washington in one of the unit's T-33s, a training plane. As I boarded the plane the pilot introduced himself, then gave me a little paper bag "just in case" my stomach acted up. It was a great thrill to feel the thrust of the jet as we taxied down the runway and then up into the sky. The pilot made a couple of loops, I am sure to see if this "pastor type" could take it, and I did!

Arrangements had been made to be met by Stan Grimm when we landed in D.C. Stan, who had been a member of our Faith Church Youth Fellowship, was now going to American University in D.C. The day we landed it was drizzling a bit so Stan met me at the airport on his motorcycle. He had brought along an extra bright yellow poncho for me to wear to the Pentagon. Remember that these were the days the entire nation was uptight about the War in Viet Nam. The Pentagon was on high alert.

Can you imagine the excitement that was raised at the Pentagon when the two of us drove up to the front door of the Pentagon, each decked out in yellow ponchos that covered our heads as well as our bodies? The paper work I carried relieved their fears of the guards. I was escorted to the proper office, interviewed and accepted, and was sworn into the NDANG as a 2nd Lieutenant.

At that time the Guard had their annual training session at Volk Field in Wisconsin and I was able to become acquainted with much of the leadership of the unit early on. My years with the Air National Guard stand out as one of the outstanding experiences of the many I had in my ministry.

I had served Faith Church for eight years. Our entire family was thoroughly enjoying the experience and the congregation was thriving.

One Sunday morning three "strangers" showed up for worship. One of them was no stranger to me however. He was the Attorney General of North Dakota, and was also a retired Methodist Pastor. I began to suspect that a change of appointment might be in order. After all, eight years in one parish in those days of Methodism was quite a long time. When the Service was ended they approached me and asked if they could speak with me. We went to the Pastor's Study in the basement of our little church and they were very forthright with me. They were members of McCabe Church in Bismarck, and they would like me to come to be the Pastor there. McCabe, at that time, was the second largest congregation in the North Dakota Conference. What an honor to be considered. But as we visited together I indicated that I felt it would be important for me to stay at Faith Church at least another year or two. Then I would certainly be open to an invitation. They accepted that, and things settled down until the next Conference year.

Daughter Laurie Elizabeth was born on June 22, 1959 – 40 minutes after Father's Day ended. I mention this particularly because some company in Fargo had promised a quarter of beef to the first child born on Father's Day. No child was born on Father's Day! But Laurie was 40 minutes late! We still tease her about this from time to time.

The year 1959 was a tough year for me personally as I lost three of the men who had meant so much to my personal development. In February the Rev. Royer Woodburn, who had been the Director of the Wesley Foundation while I was at UND was on board an American Airlines plane that went off the runway in NYC, and ended up in the East River. A handful of persons were saved, but most were drowned, and Royer was one of them. He and his family lived in Nashville, TN at the time, serving with the Methodist Television, Radio and Film Commission.

Dr. Marcus Birrell had served as President of Wesley College in Grand Forks during the years I was attending UND. I was his personal secretary for a couple of those years, but more than that, he was a close personal friend and Mentor. He also presided at our wedding. For several summers our family had used their family cabin on Lake Carlos near Alexandria, MN. In 1957 he left Grand Forks to become Secretary of the Interboard Committee on Christian Vocations in Nashville, TN. He was speaking at a meeting in Cincinnati, OH when he was stricken by a coronary thrombosis, and died very suddenly.

Then just before Thanksgiving Day my Dad had another heart attack. He was in Mercy Hospital in Valley City, ND. It appeared he was slowly recovering. Jane and I and children were having Thanksgiving Dinner at her parents' home near Wheatland. In the afternoon Jane and I went in to Valley City to visit Dad expecting to see him on the road to recovery. While we were there his death came suddenly and unexpectedly. I must say it was a holy experience for me, for as we stood by his bed he raised up in his bed as though he saw someone. Then he settled down and was gone. My Dad was such a simple man in some ways. He had only had the equivalent of a third grade education. But his wisdom ran deep, and he left a significant mark on my life. There are still some days when I feel him very close to me.

There comes to mind an experience from when I was about 15. I was working with Dad at the garage. We were testing a large truck inner tube in a tank filled with water. In those days all tires had an inner rubber tube which held the air. When it was punctured it could be mended with either a cold cement patch, or with a vulcanized patch. We were looking for the hole so it could be patched. As we stood there Dad said, "David, life is kind of like putting your finger in a pail of water." He put his finger in the tank at that time. "But when you pull it out, it isn't long and there isn't any sign that it was there at all." That has not been true of my Dad's influence on my life, and on many others as well.

Halloween of 1960 had an especially "hallowed" meaning for us this year for our fifth daughter, Christine Joanne was born. She was wildly welcomed by her four sisters. She is still sometimes razzed about being a Halloween Witch.

When Pines Reach the Sky

I remember, I remember the fir trees dark and high.
I used to think their slender tops were pressed
  against the sky.
It was a childish ignorance, but now 'tis little joy
To Know I'm further off from Heaven than when I
  was a boy.
  – Thomas Hood

In December 1960 friend Bernard Curtis invited me to go along to Bemidji, MN, to cut our Christmas tree on his property there. It proved to be a life-changing journey. When we arrived at the Curtis' property we stopped to have tea with an old bachelor, Louis Zopf, from whom Bernard had purchased his property. As we visited Louis said "I have a hundred feet of shoreline on Midge Lake, that I would sell to you for $900 today, Dave." I had no idea where I would find the $900, but before we left that day we had purchased the lots. That was the beginning of many years of relationship to the Bemidji-Cass Lake area, and a deeply enriching family experience.

In early Spring 1961 Faith Methodist Church launched into an exciting program that became a life-changing experience for a host of people. Earlier in the year the Official Board of the Church had agreed to enter into a relationship with the Methodist Board of Missions to sponsor a Cuban refugee family.

This was the year of the Cuban revolution under Fidel Castro. Although Castro's motives may have been high the process he undertook to equalize income in Cuba was demonic. The country became a communist-governed country and therefore all properties became the property of the government.

Many persons in Cuba fled the country to escape despotic control. Among them was the Jose Sotolongo family. Mr. Sotolongo had been owner of a thousand acre sugar beet compound that employed about 50 persons. With the revolution he realized that he was no longer in control, and all he had earned through his lifetime now belonged to the Cuban government. So the family decided to escape while they could. With $5 in their pocket and 5 suitcases they arrived in Florida, and through the Methodist Church were recommended to Faith Church for sponsorship. The congregation enthusiastically accepted the challenge. The local church promised to assist the family in getting housing, and finding work. The family consisted of Jose, his wife Neyda, Horacio (18) and Felipe (8). With the help of the congregation Mr. Sotolongo found work at NDAC in the Agronomy Department, and Horacio (who was the only one who could speak English) enrolled at the AC.

The language difference led to some interesting experiences. One morning Jose was asked to till a small field "kitty-korner." "What does this "kitty-korner" mean?" he asked. But through the weeks, and years, of interrelationship many lives were touched and enriched.

In June 1961 I officiated at the wedding of Jane's sister Joanne to Lloyd Reynolds of Flasher, ND. They were both graduates of Valley City State Teacher's College. The wedding was held at the Wheatland Methodist Church where Jane and I had been married.

On September 20, 1963, Dad Sheldon was taken ill very suddenly, and died before the ambulance reached the hospital. He was a well-loved man by all in the community. And he loved his grandchildren. They will miss him. The funeral was held at the Wheatland Methodist Church. I think I am correct in saying that this was the last "official" act performed at the old church. It was dismantled shortly after. All that remains of it physically for us is a rock from its foundation which is in our fireplace facing at our lake cabin.

By 1964 I had achieved the rank of Captain in the North Dakota Air National Guard. That year arrangements were made to have the summer Guard training at an airfield near Anchorage, Alaska. Alaska had experienced a very severe (9.2) earthquake on Good Friday of that Spring.

I had arranged to take the first week of the training and was flown to Anchorage in our unit's C-47, a faithful old airship which had been beautifully remodeled by the local machinists. During that week I was able to see some of the severe damage that the quake had inflicted on the area. When I completed my week the C-47 brought me back to Fargo.

During the next week the plane was taking a flight from Anchorage to Salmon Island, over a ridge of mountains. During the flight the plane disappeared off radar, and was lost somewhere in the mountains. The wreckage could not be spotted at that time. Four men were lost on the flight. This was a severe blow to the spirit of the entire unit.

Search continued for the wreckage but was not found. A memorial service was scheduled for First Lutheran Church. As Chaplain I was in charge of the service. As part of my homily I used a poem written by John Gillespie Magee, Jr., an American pilot with the Royal Canadian Air Force serving during World War II in England. Magee had written the poem just a day or two before he himself was killed in an air collision. As it was already such a significant poem in the lives of many of the pilots in the unit it seemed appropriate to use it as part of the service. It is a powerful poem:

> Oh! I have slipped the surly bonds of earth
> And danced the skies on laughter silvered wings;
> Sunward I've climbed and joined the tumbling mirth
> Of sun-split clouds – and done a hundred things
> You have not dreamed of – wheeled, soared and swung
> High in the sunlit silence. Hovering there,
> I've chased the shouting wind along, and flung
> My eager craft through footless halls of air.
>
> Up, up the long, delicious , living blue
> I've topped the wind swept heights with easy grace
> Where never lark, or even eagle flew –
> And while with silent, lifting mind I've trod
> The high untrespassed sanctity of space,
> Put out my hand, and touched the face of God.
> – John Gillespie Magee, Jr.

I had many meaningful experiences in my relationship to the men in the Guard – some humorous, and some not so humorous.

One humorous experience stands out in my mind. In my early years as Chaplain we were to interview each new person who joined the Guard. There was an information form that was to be completed. One of the questions asked at that time was "What church do you belong to?" I asked this young man the question and he replied, "I don't have to answer that question." "You are correct," I said. "You don't have to answer."

We continued with the interview and as we completed it and he was ready to go he turned and said, "May I ask you why you even asked me that question?" "Well," I said, "I'll give you as direct an answer as I can. If you were to get sucked into one of the jets out there I would like to know whom I should call." He told me which church he belonged to.

More on my experiences with the North Dakota Air Guard further along.

On November 6, 1964 our household moved from a 6 female to 1 male affair, to a little more evenly divided household with the birth of our first son, Jonathan David. On the Sunday following his birth the youth group of Faith Church celebrated the event by placing a bouquet of small pink roses on the altar, with one bright white one in the center, and a note that said "Congratulations Rev. Dave." We had certainly rejoiced in the gift of all our children, but it must be admitted there was something special about the first son.

For some years it had been my practice to go up to Midge Lake with friend Bernard Curtis to cut our Christmas tree off one of his lots. During those years I had gotten to know Louis Zopf, quite well. He was a bachelor from whom we had originally purchased our lots on Midge Lake. In April of 1965 I made a trip to Midge to see how our trailer and lots had fared through the winter. I stopped by to see Louis and have a cup of tea with him. During our conversation he said, "Dave I could sell your property here at Midge for enough money for you to buy eight lots over on Little Wolf Lake. Are you interested?" Having no knowledge of Little Wolf Lake at all I suggested we take a drive over and take a look. So we did. Little Wolf Lake is about four miles east of Midge, on a ridge that runs between two lakes: Little Wolf and Spring Lake. We drove down a trail on the top of the ridge and came to a heavily wooded part. There he asked me to stop. As I opened the door of the car to get out a bevy of wood grouse got up and flew further into the ridge woods. That was the first thing to impress me. We then investigated the beach. There was no white, sandy beach, but a drop off of about two feet to the water. But looking through the water it appeared that the lake bottom was sand.

I decided to make the change, with somewhat of a knot in my stomach. When I returned home and told the family about the trade it seemed my gut instinct was correct: they were not pleased with the decision. But as the years have gone it seems the decision was a good one after all. The trade gave us more territory on which to spread out. It also led to the purchase of the adjacent Teichmann lots and cabin, which have proved to be a real boon to our family get-togethers.

In May I was invited to accept an appointment as a District Superintendent. In the Methodist System this is considered quite a "promotion." But there seemed to be no "call of God" in it. My heart was in the local parish, and I chose to stay there, knowing that somewhere down the road I would be expected to move from Faith Church.

During that summer my Aunt Ed and Aunt Billie moved to an apartment in Valley City. So another of my boyhood places to "anchor" was gone. Even more than that. At one time there had been five Knecht families in Wimbledon. The move of my Aunts meant that now Mother was the only one left in Wimbledon. She began to make plans to rent her house and sell the store and move to Valley City also. Given her age and life-situation it was undoubtedly a smart thing to do.

Dear Aunt Ed had a rough winter and died in early Spring at the age of 84. Aunt Billie moved to a different apartment.

These two Aunts had a tremendous impact on my life. Aunt Ed (Edwina) was one of the most accepting and open-minded persons I had ever met. She worked hard all of her life on a meager salary as a bookkeeper at the local creamery, and she learned to be content. Aunt Billie (Willhelmina) spent most of her life as a missionary in Kentucky. Her faith outlook was rather narrow but she cared deeply for people. This communicated itself to me. I know she prayed that I would become a Pastor. Her prayer was answered, but I am sure she would not have appreciated my understanding and practice of the Christian Faith. I am grateful for their lives.

As I expected the year 1984 became the year of the move. I was appointed to serve McCabe Church in Bismarck – which at that time was the second largest congregation in North Dakota Methodism. I had an Associate in ministry, which was a first for me. I learned that this can be both an asset and a liability. Two of the Associates I had through our 13 years there were very effective Pastors and our friendship has endured through the years: Roger Jespersen and Phil Lint.

Because of a shuffling of several pastors in the appointments our arrival in Bismarck was not until July. This didn't give us much time to get acquainted with the congregation and start making plans for the Fall. The congregation welcomed us with open arms, and the lay leadership that was in place was committed and strong. By the time school began in September I began to have some sense of the needs and strengths of the congregation, and felt an excitement about the ministry possible there.

On Saturday, November 27, Mother had an auction sale of the store buildings and of all items within at Wimbledon. Mother was a "spunky" person and got things set up in good style. I think the sale went well, although I never did hear the final results. This was like a nail in the door, closing off the involvement of the Knecht family in the life of the village of Wimbledon. We have visited there from time to time, mainly for funerals, and I still have a warm place in my heart for the community. It has changed radically since the days that I grew up there.

We Widen Our Circle

"The test of our progress is not whether we add more to the abundance of those who have much; it is whether we provide enough for those who have little."
– Franklin Delano Roosevelt

Our family grew fast, and the girls were involved in school and church activities. One day the girls came to Jane and said, "Mother, you can't let Jon grow up alone in a family of six women. We think you ought to have another boy." She gently explained to them that she was not willing to take a chance on having five more girls to get another boy. But the conversation did get Jane and I talking about the possibility of adopting a boy.

There was an office of The Village – Family Service, from Fargo, in our Church building. I said to Jim Erickson, the Director there "If someday you get a boy to be adopted who may be difficult to place for some reason or other would you let us know?" Jim got a big smile on his face, and reaching into his coat pocket, he pulled out a picture: "I have one right now," he said. The boy was Native American from the New Town Reservation. His Mother had died of alcoholism. His grandmother was trying to raise him, but she had lost a leg because of diabetes and found it was not possible for her. The lad had some leg problems from poor nutrition in infancy. After much discussion in the family we decided to go for it. Arrangements were made, and we were to go to the Village in Fargo to receive him. On December 11, 1967, we made the trip. The boy was shy of course, but came along with us without any difficulty. He clutched tightly in his hands a furry stuffed toy cat. He has this in his possession to this day. He was welcomed into the family easily when we arrived home that evening. Jane rocked him a bit before he willingly went to bed in the room with Jon. We decided to give him the name Timothy David.

Jon welcomed Tim into his territory, and willingly shared his toys and his room. Then one day, after a week or ten days, during Tim's nap time, Jon said to Jane: "When is he going home?" Jane asked, "Who?" Jon pointed to their bedroom and said, "him." So here Tim's presence became reality. Jane patiently explained to Jon that Tim was with us to stay; that he was a new brother of his, and they would enjoy each other as he got to know Tim a bit. Life became "real." This became true quite quickly. There were the usual childhood spats, but they soon became good comrades.

Tim needed braces on his legs to help straighten them. The Shrine organization was helpful with the examination and the purchase of braces. Tim seemed to accept the braces without difficulty. He wore them about two years, but how happy he was when he could be free of them.

These were full days in every way. The girls were all in school, some involved in 4-H, some of them taking piano lessons. Jane got involved in the art community, and was taking some lessons as well as doing some painting. She was also elected to the State Board of the League of Women Voters, and because of our living in the capital city when the Legislature met the League was especially active. She also got involved in an Indian Club, with the broad commitment to help build bridges between the Indian Community and the Community of Bismarck. There was still a lot of prejudice toward the Native American Community in the city.

I was elected by the North Dakota Conference of the Methodist Church to attend the Jurisdictional Conference of the Church, which is the body that elects Bishops when there is a vacancy. The General Conference of the Church is the basic governing body of the Methodist Church and meets every four years. On the in-between 2 year schedule the Jurisdictional Conference meets for the main responsibility of evaluating Bishops and electing new ones if necessary. From this point on, until my retirement in 1986 I was elected to every General and Jurisdictional Conference – quite an honor, and a marvelous experience to see the mechanics of the church in action. This had both its good and bad sides! Human nature is human nature within the church as well as in secular society.

The McCabe Congregation continued to grow in number and in spirit. One day Dr. Duane Ewers, who at that time was Pastor of First Methodist Church in Fargo, called to tell me that McCabe was now the largest congregation in North Dakota Methodism. One of the highlights of my ministry there was the preaching ministry. I love to preach, and the congregation was responsive.

In 1955 fighting broke out in Vietnam, Laos, and Cambodia, as communism in China began to push down the peninsula. There was fear that if those countries fell to communism the rest of the world would follow as falling dominos. At the same time there was a lot of opposition to the war. Actually war was never declared. To many of us it seemed like a battle that was not ours. It stands now I think as one of the darkest times in the history of our nation. The Vietnam Memorial on the Mall in Washington is a dramatic representation of the thousands of American lives that were lost in a badly administered war. To stand at the Wall, and see the list of persons who died is one of the most moving experiences of my life.

Also during this time the John Birch Society was founded by a conservative candy manufacturer named Robert W. Welch, Jr.

It was a conservative group very outspoken in anti-communist sentiment, and the limitation of the size of government. This element became a very divisive force in our nation, and to some degree it became somewhat of a divisive factor in our congregation as well. Since my sentiments were so far in the opposite direction of some of the John Birch Society tenets I came under harsh criticism by some of the congregation. But we weathered the storm.

In every congregation you are bound to find those who are unhappy with the direction the church is going. More often than not they are religiously ultra-conservative.

I had a couple in the congregation who were quite outspoken as to how I was failing the congregation. They would often come to my office on Monday mornings to tell me all that they thought was wrong with our church. In the first place Monday morning is the most difficult morning of the week to face criticism because in the "hangover" after Sunday's sermon you are usually not too pleased with yourself anyhow.

One Monday here they came. They really lit into me, and I began to wonder whether there was anything I was doing was worthwhile. When they had finished their tirade and left I put my head on my desk and wept.

One of the strong "pillars" of the congregation was Judge George Register, a U.S. District Judge. He was a fine Christian gentleman. Besides we were in agreement on most political things! When I recovered my wits I called Judge Register and asked if he had any time I could come talk with him. "Why don't you come right now, Dave, if it's convenient for you." It was convenient for me so I went down directly, and when I was ushered into his office I broke down in tears again. He wondered what the problem was and I reported on my conversation that morning. "Oh Dave," he said, "those people have been crucifying preachers ever since I've known them." And the sun broke through the clouds. We had a good talk. He assured me that from his perspective things were going well with the church. So things came back into proper perspective.

The husband of this couple was the Chair of the Finance Committee. At one meeting of the Official Board the Board was approving expenditures. We came to the telephone bill. My "friend" started going through the long distance calls, asking to whom they were made. I think I answered two of them and then I realized that this was uncalled for. I said, "Some of those phone calls might be
Confidential situations. I refuse to answer any more. If you don't have enough faith in me to trust me to use wisely long distance calls then you have the wrong pastor." I stalked out of the room, went to the Study, and cried.

The next morning a mid-age man came in to see me. He had just joined the church so I didn't know him well We visited a while in general, and then he said, "You know, Dave, I could hardly believe my ears last night at the meeting." I thought to myself, "Oh no, not another one." Then he continued: "I never realized that Pastors had to take so damn much guff!" I knew I had another friend.

During the winter of 1969 we began to make plans for a wonderful summer. I enrolled for two six weeks sessions at the University of British Columbia, in Vancouver B.C. Two visiting professors were the attraction: John MacQuarry, a British Theologian, and an outstanding Old Testament scholar whose name I cannot remember. The University had offered to find us housing. When I reported to them that we were a family of nine this struck them with consternation, but they worked it out. A Baptist Pastor offered to rent his house to us, while he and his family took their camper and spent the six weeks in one of B.C.'s beautiful camps.

Vancouver is a beautiful city. The parsonage where we stayed was in an interesting area between an Italian community and a Japanese community. I attended classes all morning. In the afternoon we would head for the beach, or for some sight-seeing venture. Then, after the children were tucked in for the night, I would do my "homework." The children were involved in swimming lessons, and playing with the children in the neighborhood.

Oftentimes on week-ends we would go up to Stanley Park, a great place to view the city and the bay. There was a little restaurant there and we would order tea and crumpets with wonderful strawberry jam, and enjoy the view. On our last trip up there Jane mustered the courage to ask the cook if he would be willing to share his recipe for crumpets. He got a bit red in the face, went back into the kitchen, and came out with a frozen package of commercial crumpets. They were so good.

Mother Knecht flew out to spend a few days with us at Vancouver, and then we drove home through the beautiful Rockies of B.C. and Montana, visiting friends and family on the way.
When we returned to Bismarck Jane asked a tinsmith who lived across the street from us if he could make crumpet rings. He did. I fear we haven't used them many times.

On returning home I was invited to become a part of the team at the Heartview Alcoholic Treatment Center as a 5th Step Counselor. Heartview had bought the old Methodist Hospital in Mandan and at that time had a live-in treatment program. I worked with Heartview for ten years. It was a wonderful experience, and I learned as much about life, myself, and faith from the folk there as I learned in Seminary, and most of my experience to that point. The 12 steps of Alcoholic Anonymous are a great guide to what a Christian experience must involve as well.

One of the memorable friends I made in that experience was a young man whose 5th Step I had listened to. He ultimately became an effective member of the staff at Heartview. He often kidded me that I slept through his 5th Step. You know, that may be true! But it worked.

In June of 1971 I was promoted to the rank of Lieutenant Colonel. I was also transferred to State Headquarters in Bismarck. As a resident Chaplain there I did a lot of serving Army Guard units spread throughout the western part of the state. This often involving flying out to the site in one of the Guard "choppers." I thoroughly enjoyed that experience. That is rather strange too, because I am not fond of heights. But looking at the ground through the window in the bottom of the helicopter didn't bother me a bit.

At this point the United States Air Force honored me by presenting The Air Force Commendation Medal "for meritorious service." This was a humbling experience for me; as the saying goes "I was just doing my job.." Before retiring they recognized me with an Oak Leaf Cluster – a second award of the Air Force Commendation Medal.

The words on the commendation are very affirming, and I am grateful:

"Lieutenant Colonel David F. Knecht distinguished himself by meritorious service as Chaplain, 119th Fighter Group, North Dakota Air National Guard, Fargo, North Dakota, from 27 June 1956 to 2 June 1971. During this period, Colonel Knecht's outstanding professional skill, knowledge and spiritual leadership contributed materially to the overall attitude and dedication of the entire unit. His outstanding ability to communicate ideas through sermon, counseling and by personal example have gone far in assisting organizational commanders in the spiritual development of human resources. The distinctive accomplishments of Colonel Knecht reflect credit upon himself and the United States Air Force."

While at McCabe Church I had an intern program during the summer in which the Church would hire a young man or woman to work with us through the summer and so be exposed to the broad spectrum of what the parish ministry involved. These were outstanding young persons, either a Senior in High School, or a student in the first two years of college.

One of these interns was a young man who had been a part of our youth group at Faith Church in Fargo. Stanley Grimm was outstanding in every way. He also had a rather sly sense of humor which sometimes would sneak up on people and surprise them.

On this particular summer Stan and I had worked to recruit a group of Junior High Youth to go on Retreat at our Lake Cabin in Minnesota. I had left first thing in the morning with a group of the youth so I could get the camp organized before the entire crew came. Stan was in charge of the morning service. I never did get a copy of his original presentation, but apparently he did "lay it on" the congregation for not being as cooperative as they could be with the Pastor's leadership. In his usual way he did this with an edge of humor that apparently some of the congregation didn't appreciate…..at least one of them. It was the woman who, with her husband, would make regular visitations to me on Monday mornings to let me know all that was wrong with the church.

She was so incensed by his presentation that after church she called each of the parents of youth who were yet to leave for the retreat, urging them not to allow them to go. As a result we ended up with more youth coming along than had signed up originally. An appendage to that story: some 30-35 years later she came to a member of the church with a copy of Stan's original sermon. She said, "That was really a good sermon!" We humans are capable of growing in our understandings, thank our Creator.

Remembering the offer that Garrett Biblical Institute had made to me on my graduation there in 1953, I decided to go for a Doctorate Degree, not with the intention of getting involved in the academic world, but to strengthen my own skills in ministry in the local parish. Our Seminary in Kansas City, MO, St. Paul Seminary, offered that kind of Doctoral Program. The program involved having three month-long sessions in Januarys, and then a final six weeks in the summer before graduation. The program was an excellent morale booster after almost twenty years in ministry as well as a chance to feast on an excellent library, and exchange discussions with extraordinary students from all over the world, and splendid faculty members in a broad field of ministry.

I graduated with a Doctor of Ministry degree in 1976.

In the meantime my Mother had had a stroke, and could no longer care for herself. My older sister, Perne, who was a professional RN, and her husband Hartley, took her into their home in Devils Lake, and cared for her until her death in 1975. It is a rather strange experience to all of a sudden realize that one is now an "orphan," with both parents preceding them in death. Even at 50 years of age one feels the bond to one's parents; how amazing! Of course that means that I AM now the top level of the family tree as well.

During these busy days of family life Jane was elected as the President of the League of Women Voters of North Dakota. She had the mind and the interest to put in hours of concern in this capacity.

This was the year that North Dakota held a Constitutional Conference to review our state's constitution and suggest changes that might be made to provide better guidance for the state.

As a member of the League of Women Voters Jane was elected as one of the Committee members. She put in hours of work as they hammered out a new suggested Constitution. All of that labor went down the drain when the voters soundly defeated it. The months of January-March also meant Jane spent five days a week involved with the North Dakota Legislature in session, as the representative of the League of Women Voters. She gave commendable service through those months, as attested to by a letter of thanks from Governor Arthur Link.

When you're with your family most every day, the changes sneak up on you. All of a sudden our older daughters were working for hire, and then when Fall came, some went off to college. It was a wrenching experience for me when the first of our children left home. If I am honest I would have to admit it has been a wrenching experience when every single one of them left home.

As son Tim moved into adolescence we painfully became aware how his genetic background and early training had left its mark on him. We had never even heard of "fetal alcohol syndrome" until then – the effect on a child's mental and physical development when a Mother's life is soaked with alcohol.

One of the marks it leaves is that a child has little conception of consequences of their actions. There were some tough days during Tim's adolescence, when our feelings ranged from intense anger to complete frustration. At one point we contracted for counseling for Jane and I together with Tim. One of the hardest things to accept, and yet the only thing that can help, was when one of our counselors said very bluntly: "You have to let Tim sit on his own blisters." In other words, you must let him experience the consequences of his behavior. After years of struggle it is good to see Tim now, holding a steady job and maintaining manageable sobriety. He has some splendid skills, and a unique sense of humor. He is now a delight to have around.

Part of the credit for Tim's present situation is the faithfulness and trust of his brother Jon.
Even in Tim's worst times Jon maintained his trust in Tim's ability to get ahold of himself.

We had some wonderful experiences during the children's growing days with our four legged friends, both dogs and cats. Our old cat Cicero was a great comfort around the household. She lived with us for nineteen years, and then one day just wandered off to find a place to die.

Our first dog, Trieva, was given to us by a family in McCabe Church who, together with another family, raised Golden Retriever puppies. One day Jimmie Boxell called. "Rev Dave," he said, "anyone with a family the size of yours needs a dog." (Sure Jim!) But the Boxells gave us this precious little puppy, and she was a jewel. She was excellent with the children, and so easy to have around. She was very trainable. The whole family loved her so much. One night the children forgot to lock her quarters in the garage. The next morning Trieva was not around. We called the Police Department to report our loss.

The Police gave us little hope that Trieva would be found because they said several large dogs had disappeared, and it seemed that it could be the work of dog-nappers who would sell the animals they rounded up to a laboratory for research purposes or some operation such as that.

Unless one has been there it is difficult to understand the grief one can feel for a loved dog. We still talk about the joy that Trieva brought into our lives.

We weren't without a dog for long, however. Daughter Chris had some contact with a friend who had some puppies of a mix of collie and German shepherd. She was a beautiful dog. We took her into our family circle. We called her Madchen, which is German for "young woman." She was a friendly dog with a lot of enthusiasm. But she was a barker, and it soon became apparent that if we were going to live in peace with our neighbors Madchen would have to go We found a farmer friend from the congregation who welcomed her willingly and Madchen appreciated the new freedom.

Again it was not long before we had another dog. Once more it was Chris who first spotted a little Lhasa Apso puppy at one of her friend's home. With her large, pleading eyes Chris persuaded us to try again. We called her Tib'et, after Tibet. She was a cuddly little thing. It didn't take her long to win the hearts of the whole family.

Mother Sheldon lived with us the last six months of her life. She and Tibet had become close friends. One reason that was true, I am sure, was because she would slip "people food" to Tibet at the table. We would Grandma put a bit of food by her plate and quietly push it over the edge of the table to Tibet. Again and again we would say, "Mother, it's not good for Tibet to have "people food." "Oh no" she would say, "I wouldn't do that."

In her last days of life, a week or so before Christmas, our family made plans to meet at Mother Sheldon's room and sing Christmas Carols. It was agreed that we would all meet there, and Jane and I went ahead. The troops arrived shortly after. Here came Margaret into the room with her coat slung over her arm. It was a cold night. She revealed that she had snuck Tibet into the hospital for Mother to have one last hug of her. We convinced the ward nurse that we would just sing a few Carols and be on our way. When the nurse was out of sight Marg placed Tibet on Mother's bed, and immediately she snuggled in beside her. They were both so very happy.

Tibet gave our whole family many wonderful years of enjoyment.

Given the necessary chores of caring for a pet I doubt that we will ever have another. Instead I look out our front window at all the people from the apartment across the street, standing out in the bitter cold and wind waiting for their pet to take care of their business. It is a good occasion to say a simple prayer: "Thank you God that I don't have to stand outside on a day like this waiting for a dog to carry on his elimination process."

To Serve the Present Age

" To serve the present age, my calling to fulfill.
O may it all my powers engage to do my Master's will."
– Charles Wesley

1976 was a big year in our family history.

In the first place it was the 200th Anniversary of the United States. There were celebrations across the country of course, and our own state of North Dakota planned some significant celebrations in conjunction with the nation's celebration.

This was the year of our 25th Wedding Anniversary. Can it really be possible? In celebration of this Jane and I took a camping trip to Riding Mountain National Park on Lake Catherine near Brandon in Canada for four wonderful days. The children had decked out our car for the trip with a sign on the back that said: "Just Married – Twenty Five Years Ago." To complete their part of their celebration they tied a string of cans under our car, so as we took off from the front of the house we set out with a real jingle. I stopped around the corner and untied the cans before arousing the interest of the whole city of Bismarck on the way out of town.

This was also the year of my celebration of 25 years in the ministry. This celebration was topped off with my passing my oral exams for The Doctor of Ministry Degree from St. Paul Seminary in Kansas City. On the 17th of May at a ceremony in the St. Paul Chapel my own Bishop James Armstrong had a part in putting the Doctoral hood over my head. The entire family made the trip to Kansas City to have a part in that celebration.

In addition to this celebration I was again elected by the ND Annual Conference to our denomination's General Conference, this year in Portland OR, and to the Jurisdictional Conference in Sioux Falls, SD. One of the issues that began emerging at the General Conference was he presence of the Lesbian and Gay contingent appealing to our denomination for recognition of them as children of God and earnest disciples of Jesus Christ. There were many in the Conference that were not even willing to give them the "time of day." I had not given the issue much thought because I had never had friends or acquaintances whom I knew to be gay or lesbian. Since then I have watched our culture struggle with the issue, and I know where I am at. They are people who didn't choose their sexual orientation, just as I didn't choose mine. They need to be allowed the freedom to be who they are.

Two of the highlights of a work that Jane and I did together throughout North Dakota and beyond, was leading PET (Parent Effectiveness Training) sessions and leading Marriage Enrichment Retreats. We were both trained in the content of both disciplines and it was stimulating to be able to share with other younger couples some of the skills they could develop to strengthen their relationship to each other, and to feel good about their relationships with growing children. Both of these disciplines seem to have been shadowed by the uncertain times in which we live, just when they are probably needed as more or maybe even more than ever.

In February 1977 I attended three weeks of training for Guard Chaplains at the Air Base in Montgomery, Alabama. It was cold, even for one from North Dakota. My roommate was also from "north of the Mason-Dixon Line." After a couple of nights of trying to sleep in a cold room we mischievously slipped some ice cubes from the dining hall into a plastic bag, and tied it over the thermostat in our room. That took care of the problem effectively. This was a great experience of relationship with military chaplains from all over the world. We were also taught skills in effectively counseling with military personnel with particular problems.

About this time I was awarded the North Dakota Legion of Merit Award by Governor Allen Olson, and Adjutant General Alexander R. Macdonald.

The award, mounted on a beautiful wooden plaque, states:

"The Governor of North Dakota takes pride in presenting the North Dakota Legion of Merit to Lieutenant Colonel David F. Knecht….. For superior duty performance during the period 12 September 1964 through 10 August 1984 while serving as Chaplain for the North Dakota Air National Guard. Lieutenant Colonel Knecht has unselfishly provided his expertise and experience to all the "Happy Hooligans" of the 119th Fighter Interceptor Group. His talent as a public speaker has provided unit personnel with diverse, well prepared, articulate sermons. His written messages, published in the unit's monthly newsletter, have been a source of inspiration, projecting his positive, contagious attitude. Lieutenant Colonel Knecht aggressively approaches every responsibility with unqualified enthusiasm and his outstanding record of accomplishments, both military and civilian, attests to his efficiency, organizational ability, and impervious personal dedication."

Is any human being up to that? Whether it's true or not I don't know, but it's a great morale booster anyhow. I am grateful for the opportunity to serve my beloved America with what I have to give.

In the meantime Jane had renewed her teaching certificate and served as a para-professional at Northridge School in Bismarck helping fifth and sixth graders in need of organizational, motivational or academic help. This was both a frustrating and a fulfilling experience for her. In addition to this she continued as President of the League of Women Voters and was involved in another session of the ND Legislature.

One of the issues that was to be considered by the Legislature was adding the Mourning Dove to the game bird category to be hunted. One of Jane's uncles, Paul, was deeply opposed to this issue, and enlisted Jane's assistance in contacting all of the legislators, encouraging them to defeat the issue. She prepared a leaflet in this regard and placed it on every Legislator's desk. In spite of these efforts the issue passed. I have often wondered how many "glorious hunters" engage themselves in hunting one of the quietest and most beautiful of North Dakota native birds, especially considering what a meager amount of "meat" each bird could provide.

In January 1978 Mother Sheldon left us, and we celebrated her life. Florence Medland Sheldon had attended the University of North Dakota. She was an accomplished pianist, but did not manifest her skills very widely. She was a quiet person, but had her deep personal life. She taught school in her early years of life, and then later for a short term at Bathgate and Oberon. While teaching in Wheatland she met and married Charles Sheldon. They spent most of their life together farming in the Wheatland area. She was an only child and was devoted to taking care of her parents when they needed a place of help in their old age. She gave herself completely to her family, Jane, Bill and Joanne, and her husband. For much of her life she lived on a farm not equipped with all the accouterments of easy living. We were grateful for the few months she became a resident part of our family before she died.

It came time for daughter Chris' Senior year at Bismarck High School. She was chosen as Queen of her class, and in this our family rejoiced. She had also performed as a cheerleader for Bismarck High during her years there. She was and is a delightful person who is enjoyed by all.

This was the year of our first exchange pulpit in England. The Methodist Church at that time had a program where a Pastor could exchange pulpits and responsibilities with a Pastor in another part of the world.

We worked out an exchange with Les and Allison Judd, citizens of England. They had served Methodist Churches in North Dakota for a short time, and we got to know them well. Les was now serving churches in northern England, at Gateshead and Sheriff's Hill, in Tyne and Ware. Flying to England we passed each other somewhere in the skies. The Judd's took our place at McCabe Church while we served Les' two churches in England. A local travel agency worked out our travel plans. We landed at Heathrow Airport outside of London. I had arranged for the rental of a small "Caravan," a European style self-contained camper. Our first need was to go to Brighton, outside London, pick up the camper, and drive (on the left side of the highway) up to Gateshead, just a few miles short of the Scottish border.

All of the children accompanied us over, and then after spending a short week with us the three older girls had to return to Bismarck for work responsibilities. The people of Gateshead and Sheriff's Hill were so receptive to us. We were also able to do some sight-seeing in the English northland. The people of Gateshead apologized to us for being on the "edge" of England. They said, "People in England say this is not the end of the world, but you can see it from here."

"Interesting," I said. "People of the U.S. say that about us in North Dakota also." We spent five weeks in Gateshead and made some very dear friends there. We were also able to visit a college "pen pal" of Jane's, who lived at "The Haven, Out Elmstead Lane, Near Canterbury, York, England."

After fulfilling our responsibilities at Gateshead we took our little camper (Gus, we called it) across the Channel and spent about three weeks to making a loop around Europe: France, Liechtenstein, Switzerland, Germany, Austria, Luxemburg, Belgium and the Netherlands. We prize an Anniversary candle that we made by melting all the candles involved in our wedding into one large candle. We had our Anniversary Candle along and stopped to celebrate with dinner at Aachen, just before crossing into Belgium. We asked the waitress if we could light our candle. She asked us what it signified, so we told her it was in commemoration of our wedding anniversary. We had a delightful dinner, and then just as dessert was served to us a roving violinist came to our table and played for us "The Anniversary Waltz." Beautiful!

We drove back to London, turned in our little camper, which gave us minor problems from time to time, and took a cab back to Heathrow Airport. What a surprise! Our travel agent had given us our date of departure, but had not made a reservation for us. So there we were, all six of us, anxious to get home, and no reservation. I inquired of British Airways whether any reservations were available. None! What could we do? "Well you can sign up for standby." "Six of us!" "How did we go about that?" "You have to go to our offices in downtown London." "What!" That would have been impossible.

I had turned in all of the variety of monies we had collected across Europe. We arranged to stay at a nearby Holiday Inn for the night. I was able to book Budget Fare passage on a plane home the next week. Fortunately I had enough money left to do this. The Judds were so gracious, and put all of us up for a week until our day of departure. So we were on hand that day, boarded our plane, and settled in for the ride home. We were amazed that we had enough money left to do this.

We flew to Minneapolis, and then on home to Bismarck. As we came to our front door there was a telegram taped to the door. I opened it immediately. The message was that the currency exchange agent at Heathrow had made a mistake. She gave us over $700 too much!

In the relief of being home we decided not to even think about it until the next morning. First thing in the morning I called one of the members of the parish who was the President of one of the local banks. I told him of our predicament. "Well," he said, "you are under no obligation, except your own moral concern, to return the money to them. It was their error." Of course that was not a solution for us, so we arranged with our friend to get the money off to the exchange agency, and fulfill our obligations. But had not that woman made that mistake, who knows, perhaps we would still be in England awaiting a "standby" ride home!

Around Christmas rumors began to circulate that we would be moving after the next Annual Conference. This was confirmed when the Cabinet came to us and invited me to return to Fargo as the Superintendent of the Eastern District of the Church. We thought it time to accept the invitation. The family had mixed feelings about this. It would mean the loss of their "home port" for those who were going away to college, or who were working in the Bismarck area. It seemed the right time to move before the boys entered Junior High. It was difficult wrapping up the year, saying many goodbyes, and then at last packing up for a return to Fargo. Our years at McCabe Church had been so rewarding to us, and I felt good about the state of the congregation we were leaving.

We moved in June to 1246 N. Oak Street. As Superintendent of the Eastern District I became overseer to 58 congregations and Pastor to 40 Pastors and their families. It would mean being on the road a lot of the time, up and down the eastern end of North Dakota. With the changing face of the church, and the many new challenges facing Pastors, such as children with special needs, or clergy couples, it seemed like a challenging call to me.

It was a challenging call. I have to admit the administrative side of the Church has never been a very satisfying one to me, but I recognize how important it is in the functioning of the church, and I felt I had some skills that might be helpful.

On September 1 we returned to McCabe to officiate in the wedding of our daughter Margaret, to Scott Schaar. Margaret had been working as a Social Worker out of Linton, ND. Scott was a Dentist in Linton. There they had met, and the magic of romance took control. It was a joy to have a part in this first child to be wed, and Scott is such a super person.

From November 25-December 5 Jane and I led a TWA guided tour of the Holy Land involving 15 other persons. This was a mixed experience for me. On the one hand it was very meaningful to see and experience places we had read about in the Bible and talked about for years. On the other hand, some of the filthy sites we visited, and places that were promoted as authentic sites of Jesus' life experiences, were a disillusioning experience for me. But overall it was meaningful to share the experience with other Christian people, and to talk together about the significance of what we saw and heard.

The life of the family was in flux at this time: college beginnings, new work beginnings, all kinds of new experiences that tested all of us in some ways. Jane and I began some counseling with ourselves and Tim, helping him deal with some of the issues of his life. As I look back on it from this perspective, it was a growing and testing time for all of us. We were each given the strength we needed, thankfully.

In the concluding months of our time in Bismarck Jane was chosen for the Judicial Qualifications Nominating Committee. The task of the Committee was to nominate persons for judgeships in vacant districts, from the names that were appointed by the Chief Justice, the State Bar Association and the Governor, who at that time was Arthur Link. It was a Committee of no small matter. After their work was completed a personal letter from Governor Link commended Jane for her admirable part in the Committee's work. Attaway Jane!

When we were settled in our routine in Fargo Jane decided she would like to go back to school and get her Master's Degree in Counseling and Guidance. After checking with NDSU she discovered she could do it by taking two courses a quarter for two years, so she signed up. Concerned about paying her own way she first took a job with Shotwell Greenhouse, which was only six blocks south of our Oak Street home. Her job was to transplant thousands of tiny seedlings to larger planters. When this job ended in the Spring she got a job with the north Broadway McDonalds. Discovering that the people who handled the money were also handling food she let her concerns be known and the managers changed their money-handling process. Attaway Jane!

All of this preparation became a part of another development. Jane and two other women with counseling qualifications started The Discovery Counseling and Educational Center. Jane worked together with them for three years until the time for my retirement approached. She proved to be very effective in her counseling skills.

What's a Family For?

"You can kiss your family and friends goodbye and put miles between you, but at the same time you carry them with you in your heart, your mind, your stomach, because you do not just live in a world, but a world lives in you."
– Frederick Buechner

The year 1980 proved to be another of shifting "tectonic plates" again in the life of our entire family. Jeanne and Jeff Johnson were married at Jeff's home farm in an outdoor service. My Aunt Billie died in April – the last of the Jacob Knecht family – the family of my Dad. I was elected to another session of the General Conference of the Methodist Church, which met this year in Indianapolis. The girls were on the move to new jobs, new locations, now activities. It was a beehive of activities.

In the midst of all of the commotion we managed a week-long canoe trip to the Boundary Waters with our friends, the Fikes. This was an outstanding experience of dealing with the hardships of the wilderness, with each of our own personal responses to that, with our life in community together – and always with the impending company of black bears. Everyone should have this unforgettable experience.

Jane had some new experiences also: A Women's Theology Conference in Aberdeen and a Conference on Families with Leon and Antoinette Smith, extraordinary leaders in the area of Marriage. After this the two of us co-led a local Marriage Enrichment Retreat with Duane and Helen Ewers.

With all of the "comings and goings" our lives were swimming in an exciting stream of activities that stretched out our minds, spirits, and experiences. Jon began High School at North High, and Tim began 9th Grade at Ben Franklin. It was almost a relief when Fall came and we could settle down into some kind of schedule again.

How could I forget that two family traditions ended this year: putting out Easter baskets for the children, and the children putting out their shoes for Santa! The Dance moves on.

I was beginning to get my feet on the ground as a District Superintendent. The process of counseling Pastors in their ministry was fulfilling. The most difficult part was the making of appointments in the Spring of each year, knowing that each family's future was about to be radically changed as they took up ministry and community life in a new place. And churches could be radically changed as well under the leadership of a new Pastor. I was thankful for the personal dimension in each of these activities, knowing all the time that the administrative dimension was important as well.

It came as a surprise when our newly appointed Bishop Edwin C. Boulton invited me to come on board as his Administrative Assistant after two years on the District. Dr. Don Klarup, who had begun at the position and had accomplished the difficult job of setting up a new Episcopal office, moved on to become Pastor of First Church in Sioux Falls. As the Bishop explained the new job to me he suggested that basically he would be out and about in the Area of North and South Dakota. It would be my job, as Ed put it, to "stay at home and sit on the eggs." As it turned out the job was more than that. One of the major responsibilities was editing the Area newspaper which was sent to every church and pastor every month (?). As well as the Bishop, I went about throughout the area with various responsibilities. I was grateful for this as it gave me a chance to get acquainted with the pastors on the South Dakota side of line.

My six years as Administrative Assistant were memorable years for me, especially working with Ed Boulton. Ed was not only a capable administrator but a source of life and joy. We became close friends through those years of ministry together. Ed had health problems most of his adult life, but he conquered them well, and the inspiration of his spirit was a gift and model for each one who knew him.

One of the difficult glitches in our family was Jeanne and Jeff's divorce. As I had counseled with them before marriage I raised questions as to whether they were ready for this step in their lives, but as with most youth "they knew better." In the wake of their divorce Jeanne joined the Air Force, which turned out to be a real asset in the future turns in the road of her future.

There was another "significant first" in our lives. Sarah Jane Schaar was born to Margaret and Scott – the first of our ten grandchildren. This beautiful little long-haired baby continues to affect our lives in many significant ways. With her marriage down the road to Scott Flores, they gave to us the gift of our first GREAT grandchild as well.

I joined the Roughrider Kiwanis Club in 1982, the beginning of a long and meaningful experience of the Kiwanis spirit and brotherhood. I will talk about this a bit later on.

About this time our adopted son Tim was experiencing real struggle in his own life with chemical dependency. This led to some difficulties with the law and a bit of time in prison. After several attempts at sobriety he ended up in residential treatment in Jamestown, and this proved to be most helpful to him. He had been through a treatment program at St. Mary's in

Minneapolis before, and he had received the medal of sobriety, but it didn't get to the heart of things. In talking with Tim later about this he thought maybe it was because all of the youth he was involved with in that program came from upper class homes. He had nothing in common with them. In the healing process at Jamestown we had discovered that Tim's birth father would like to have a chance to meet him. Arrangements were made with Social Service and we drove to New Town, and a chance for Tim to meet with his birth father, George Lewis. It was an emotional meeting for them, and also for us as you can imagine. Tim chose to stay with him on the Reservation for a while, and there he had the opportunity to meet many of his relatives. But after a time he called to say that he wanted to come "home." "It's like a jungle up here," he said. Although the whole experience was a difficult one for all of us I think it helped Tim discover who he is as a person in his own right. There is a sense in which his discovery process is still going on, as it is for all of us. It was part of his journey to sobriety. He is at a different place now.

My sister Karen had been struggling with balance difficulty and walking for some time. After intense examination it was indicated that she had a growing brain tumor. She was treated with radiation therapy but nothing could seem to stop the tumors continuing growth. She died on December 22, 1980. To have one of one's siblings die brings an entirely different perspective on the reality of death. I have reminded myself many times: "When one is old enough to be born one is old enough to die." Karen's death was particularly difficult for her husband Jim. Jim had never been a very social person. He enjoyed his family and his close circle of friends. He had had a very rough tour of duty in the army, particularly during the battle for Iwo Jima. The mental stress was so great he had spent time in a military hospital. The loss of Karen, who was in a sense his "gateway" to the world, was a blow he never recovered from up to his death in 2014.

While our months as a District Superintendent were packed with travel, both for professional purposes, and as family. I led a travel trip to England with a group of 15 persons, to follow the footsteps of Methodist's founder, John Wesley. The group stayed with people from the local church, which proved to be a highlight of the trip for all, including the locals. Jane and I led another group trip a couple of years later. England is a beautiful country, and the people were so receptive to us. We continue contact with a few of them still, but time has taken its toll on most.

Boyhood friend, LeRoy Meier, one of the Tragic Trio, died very suddenly on May 18, 1988. It is a very different experience to lose a close friend, near one's own age, and an older relative, even one's parents. Youth, I know, have a sense that they will live forever, but I experienced that this feeling goes on later in our life. Sixty-four is too young to die! My heart had a difficult time accepting that. LeRoy was really the first of close friends to die. This has ramifications for oneself. There comes the awareness that when one is born one is old enough to die. To acknowledge that is to take another leap in the dance of life. And I was now entering the era of life when anything can happen to any of us.

As a Pastor, even the acknowledgement of the ashes of the Good Friday service began to come "home" with a powerful punch: "Dust thou art; to dust thou shalt return." Somewhere in life everyone must begin to recognize that fact.

Son Jon had made an attempt at going to College, enrolling in NDSU, but it was obvious after a few weeks that he was not ready to settle down in college. He found work he enjoyed, first at Leeby's Market on north Broadway, and then with Dakota Fence in Fargo.

How surprised I was one day when I came home to find him talking to a young man from Dakota Wesleyan University at Mitchell, SD. Before their conversation ended, Jon had signed up for Dakota Wesleyan, and began school that week. There he found good friends, and more personal relationships with faculty. The classes were smaller, and this seemed to fit his style.

He graduated from Dakota Wesleyan. While there he had made the discovery that he had a wonderful talent in the art field. Before he graduated he was allotted the Art museum display room for a show of his own. His continuation in his development of art has been a source of great enjoyment to him and of great pride to us through the years.

In 1987 I was invited to give the Baccalaureate Sermon at Dakota Wesleyan, and during the Graduation Program I was awarded an Honorary Doctor of Divinity degree. It was a great honor to be recognized by the University in this way, but I have always been sensitive about a "Doctoral Degree," even when I earned another scholastically. To me it seems like a pretentious thing to claim the title for myself. On the other hand I have a friend from Seminary days who almost insists that he be addressed as "Doctor." Somehow that doesn't square with my concept of discipleship with Jesus, "the human one," as a modern translation of the Gospels interprets him. To me the doctoral program became another route to improve my personal skills of ministry.

As I began to anticipate my leaving the Area Office as Administrative Assistant, and my retirement from active ministry in a short four years I suggested to Bishop Boulton that I would like to be assigned to a small congregation for those last four years in order to just slow down. You can almost guess what happened. He made an appointment for me to meet with the Staff Parish Committee of old First Church in Fargo to see if they would accept me there! Of course they did. Cameron Johnson, who had served that church well for several years took my position in the Area Office and I became the Senior Pastor of Fargo First Church.

Although the thought of taking on that kind of responsibility at 61 was rather daunting, it turned out to be an exciting time. Richard Teichmann, who had been a youth in our days at Faith Church, was named the Associate Pastor. Dick was a good man to work with.

First Church in Fargo was the very first Methodist Episcopal Church in the Dakotas Territory that became "North" Dakota. It had a long heritage of powerful ministry and outstanding preachers. However, the years had taken a toll. It was a very proud parish, which is both good and bad. It was obvious to me on first sight that some changes needed to be made.

After my first session with the Administrative Board I recognized that for one thing meetings needed be planned more effectively. That meeting lasted about 2 ½ hours, to get at best an hour's work done. The members of the Board loved to visit but the visiting was interspersed with the business so a lot of time was taken up to get little done. At our second meeting I suggested to them that we aim for an hour long meeting, and then stay as long afterward as anyone wanted to visit. That worked out well. The visiting was an important part of being a community of Faith, but it distracted much during the time of business.

Another immediate impression on me was the condition of the old building. There was no elevator to go between the four levels of the building and many members of the congregation were aged. The classrooms for Christian Education were dingy with ragged carpet and shabby paint. There are advantages to come to a new assignment on the verge of retirement for one can afford to be blunt without fear of losing one's job! I said at one meeting "If I had small children I would hesitate to send them to church school in this building." Surprising to me there were members of the Board who readily agreed with me. After the meeting I was visiting with a couple of men of the Board. They indicated that they had been anxious to make some changes for a long time, but nothing happened. I said, "Why don't one of you make a motion that something be done?" At a future meeting such a motion was made, and after some discussion, the motion passed unanimously, and machinery was set in motion to attack the changes that needed to be made.

It was a thrilling experience. A financial emphasis was organized, and the pledges needed came in. A building committee was named and plans were developed for renovating the building, including an elevator, and renovation of the church school building. Partitions in the old White Hall were torn out, the outer wall was secured. A beautiful stained glass window that had been covered up for decades was uncovered. Many of the congregation didn't even know it existed. On my part it was not a matter of saying, "get going." It was almost a matter of saying "slow down." The four years that I spent in ministry there were exciting years, although I must admit that pastoral matters were not the prime focus in the midst of deconstruction and construction. It was a great experience to finish up my ministry.

Finish up my ministry? I was in midst of my last year there when I received a call from Bishop William Lewis. "Dave, we're having some problems at McCabe Church in Bismarck. The Cabinet would like you to consider going there for a year as an interim pastor to get things settled down."

What a bomb! One of the members of the Cabinet was so sure I would say "No" that he bet a year's salary (in jest) with another of the Cabinet. After prayerful consideration, and talking with the Tannehills, a beloved retired Pastor and wife who had spent years of fruitful ministry at McCabe, and prayer , we told the Bishop we would go. As we visited with the Tannehills about our possibility of coming back for a year, we asked them whether they thought we could be helpful. I will never forget the answer of Cecelia Tannehill: "Dave, all we need is someone to love us." Well, love them we could and did.

Rumor had it that the trouble in the congregation was with the choir. Jane joined the choir, the first time in our ministry together, to see what the trouble was. There was no trouble there. The "trouble" disappeared when the former pastor and his spouse moved on to another appointment. We had a wonderful time with the congregation through that year. The difficulty of an interim pastorate is that you don't have the freedom to plan for the future as you will not be there to see it through.

In April sometime, I had heard that Bishop Lewis was coming to Bismarck to preach at First Church. I called him, "Bishop, here it is April already and I have not heard of anyone coming to be the Pastor of McCabe Church." "Well Dave," he replied in his rather high pitched voice, "we were hoping you'd be willing to stay another year." "No Bishop," I boldly responded, 'I promised you a year, and the year is up in June." After a bit more visiting he could see that our mind was made up. An excellent Pastor was sent in to pick up the ministry there.

Annual Conference arrived, and a part of the "business" of the Conference is to pass on the retirement of those who request retirement and are eligible. So now in June we had completed almost fifty years in the ministry. It had been a great "dance." We had worked with so many wonderful people. We had seen lives changed and new directions set. We ourselves had grown, and now stood at a different place in our lives. We felt we could move on.

Our last service at First Church was a glorious celebration with special music, guests from former parishes, and the announcement that a Scholarship Fund had been created at Garrett-Evangelical Theological Seminary in the name of Jane and myself. What an honor! We are still adding to that scholarship, and have now seen three young persons receive the benefit of it during their schooling there.

The Fullness of Life

"Never make your home in a place. Make a home for yourself inside your own head. You'll find what you need to furnish it – memory, friends you can trust, love of learning, and other rich things. That way it will go with you wherever you journey."
– Ted Williams

There are several other issues that might come into our story at this point.

1. The Masonic Lodge

I have been a member of the Kiwanis Club for many years, joining for the first time with the Roughrider Club in Fargo in 1980. I admire the stated Objectives of Kiwanis:

1. To give primacy to the human and spiritual rather than to the material values of life.
2. To encourage the daily living of the Golden Rule in all human relationships.
3. To promote the adoption and the application of higher social, business and professional standards.
4. To develop, by precept and example, a more intelligent, aggressive and serviceable citizenship.
5. To provide, through Kiwanis Clubs, a practical means to form enduring friendships, to render altruistic service and to build better communities.
6. To cooperate in creating and maintaining that sound public opinion and high idealism which make possible the increase of righteousness, justice, patriotism, and goodwill.

I was privileged to serve as President of the Roughriders before we left for service at McCabe Church in Bismarck. I also put in two years as the Roughrider Treasurer. I belonged to the Bismarck Kiwanis all the time we were in Bismarck, and was President of that Club for one term. This experience gave me the opportunity to get to know persons of many walks of life, and many different backgrounds, whom I would not have met in any other way.

When we moved back to Fargo I joined up with the Roughriders again. I determined that if they would have me I would stay until I was 80 years old. When I became 80 I resigned from the Roughriders and went to visit the Golden K Club. It took one meeting for me to determine that I wasn't quite ready for that so I went back to the Roughriders to see if they would have me at my age. Of course they would. Intentions now are to try to stay until 90!

2. The Big Brother Program

Another rich dimension of my life was becoming a Big Brother in the program of the Village Family Service. I was assigned a little brother, Corey Mertz, who was six at the time. His mother was raising a family of three boys and one girl by herself. Corey and I did many different activities together, but a favorite for him, and for me as well, was to make the trip to our lake cabin for a couple of days. While we were there on one trip he caught his very first fish. This was a real thrill to him, and to me. Cory loved loud music and professional wrestling, neither of which were on my agenda, but I learned from it.

A great friend of mine from First Church was Jack Thompson. His one daughter was divorced, and she had a boy and a girl. Jack was really the father figure for her son Nic as he grew. Jack died very suddenly, which left a gaping hole in the life of young Nic., who was about 10 or 12 years old at the time. His Mother called me to see if I had any ideas of what she might do to give him some male influence. I suggested she call the Big Brother program. She called back in a couple of days to say there were almost 200 boys on the waiting list! "Well," I said, "let me check with the Big Brother program. If they have no objections and my little brother Corey has no objections, I will take Nic as another little brother." And that is the way it turned out. It was a wonderful experience because whereas Corey enjoyed loud music and professional wrestling, Nic was a classical music lover, and a gentle person by nature. The great thing was that even with their differences they enjoyed each other. And both of them enjoyed trips to the Haven. Both boys have since moved on into their adult lives of course. I understand Corey has a family and lives in Valley City. I never hear from him. But Nic and I now have a beautiful friendship – a young man with a growing family, and an old man whose family is grown. The Big Brother-Big Sister program is a real winner as far as I am concerned.

While I was Pastor at Fairmount one of the members of the parish was elected the Grand Master of the Masonic Lodge of North Dakota. He had convinced me to join the Masonic Lodge, and I did, partly because it was basically my "Men's Club." Most of the members of the Lodge were members of our congregation. I was reluctant to join the Lodge for two reasons. In the first place I felt I had enough "plates in the air" to keep me as busy as I cared to be. In the second place, Jane had no love for the Masons. As we talked about that, her underlying feeling came out of an experience her Dad had of being "blackballed" for admission to the Lodge. Before one can join a Lodge they are to be voted on by the members of the Lodge. Voting was done as each member was given two small "balls" - marbles – one black and one white. If they were in favor of admitting the person they put the white ball in the box. If they were not in favor of admitting them they placed their black ball in the box. From that ancient practice comes the often-used term: to be "black balled." Apparently someone in the Lodge cast a black ball for Charlie and that was enough to block the door for him.

The year that John Barner was Grand Master he chose me to be his Grand Chaplain. Aside from responsibilities at the annual meeting of the Grand Lodge there wasn't much expected of me. I must admit I was not particularly comfortable in the position, partly because of Jane's feelings, and partly because I do not particularly enjoy the "formal" dimensions of the relationship.

Years later when we were in Bismarck, a member of our congregation there was elected as Grand Master. He also invited me to be Grand Chaplain with him.

I want to give this positive assessment of the Masonic Lodge: Although some of the ritual is quite puerile in my estimation, some of it is also very beautiful and moving. I was also able to see through the years that the experience of being a part of the fellowship of a local Lodge, and the discipline of learning the ritual, and having to share it before the body, was an excellent gateway for some men to grow in social graces, and their own sense of self-worth. The history of the Masonic Lodge, as well, is not to be overlooked. Through the centuries it has played a positive part in the human struggle to discover and establish freedom.

3. The Experience of Retirement

So now comes Retirement, and another major shift in the tectonic plates of my life – or to put it in other words, "a new dance." For fifty years I had a vocation to practice, to develop and grow in and a group of people to know, to serve, to enjoy. Now suddenly we have no congregation. For all of our ministry we had lived in provided housing, and now we had no permanent place to live. For all these years we had a community of faith to give us inspiration and support. Now we were without such a community.

I have had friends who were intensely terrified of the thought of retirement. I am convinced that for some of them their work had been such a most significant part of their lives that retirement had quite literally taken their "life" away. Some, I am sure, came to early death because of this. Well my work had certainly been a significant part of my life, but it wasn't the ONLY part. We had our growing family, in whom we took such great joy. I had several hobbies that I wanted to pursue. Jane and I wanted more freedom to go places and do things that we couldn't do within the confines of regular responsibilities. We had our Haven, our lake place, that we looked forward to spending some quality time developing and enjoying.

But we quickly discovered there was another dimension. I feel like paraphrasing a famous saying of General Douglas MacArthur: "old pastors never die; they just fade away." I had so many opportunities to fill in for Pastors, or to actually serve as an interim pastor in some cases. These were enjoyable without exception, but they did "disrupt" retirement plans. I served as part time interim pastor for the Ada-Beltrami parish of the United Methodist Church in Minnesota; for the Fargo Moravian Church – Shepherd of the Prairie; for the Friendship United Methodist Church on the south side of Fargo. All of these experiences widened our circle of experiencing dozens of wonderful new friends and opportunities for service. I must admit there have been times I have felt it probably would have been good to go off some place where nobody knew who we were, and thereby be free of any need to accept such opportunities. But I am grateful for each of these experiences, and for the joy they brought to our lives.

Jane and I have both been gifted with good health – and that continues now in our late eighties. Part of this, I am sure, is because we have tried to care for our bodies as best we can, and have had regular check-ups from time to time to see that we are on the right track.

4. Our health.

After we moved to Fargo we began our health relationships with Merit Care Health, associated with the old St. Luke's Hospital. My general Doctor was Dr. Frank Sepe. Not only did he have a genuine concern about his patients, but was very personable to deal with. After one of my annual physicals and related lab tests, Dr. Sepe called and said he wanted to talk with me. During our consultation he shared with me that my blood tests indicated I should look more deeply into my condition, and he recommended I have a bone biopsy. Of course I consented. The tests revealed that I had mild non-Hodgkin's lymphoma! That was a shaker! I had ministered to many persons who had battled with cancer in many forms, and with several when they could no longer win the battle. Now it was certain I had cancer!

When I went to bed that night I was surprised that my feelings were not more intense than they were. As I lay there thinking about it, it was just as though someone had audibly spoken to me: "It will be alright." I am sure there was no audible sound that someone else could have heard, but it was real to me, and a deep peace settled over me. I felt God's gracious care held me.

My records were transferred to the Roger Maris Cancer Center. I was assigned to an Oncologist, Dr. Ana Gaba. Dr. Gaba is a very caring person. Further tests were done, and she consulted with me as to possible courses of treatment. It was decided that I was to have about three months of chemo treatments, and then further testing. The treatments were 3-4 hours in length, three days a week. Essentially, as someone suggested to me, what the chemo is trying to do is "kill" the infected cells in my blood. The treatments were painless; the chemical treatment was made gradually by intravenous infusion. The overall effect on me was sheer exhaustion. There were intermittent blood tests as treatment progressed. When the treatment was completed I was limp as a rag, but the testing gave assurance that progress had been made. At this stage I still have biennial testing by my oncologist, and all tests so far are positive. I asked my oncologist what the state of the lymphoma is. She indicated that it is always there, but inactive, and it may stay that way for the rest of my life. I am thankful first of all for Dr. Sepe's astute diagnosis, and then for the continuing care I experience through the Roger Maris Cancer Center and Dr. Gaba. So many who come that way are not as fortunate as I have been.

5. Jane's activities.

In the last years of our ministry, my darling wife was a very active woman. She should tell her own story here. For example, she and two other women had founded the Discovery Counseling and Education Center, as indicated earlier. Jane was with Discovery for six years, doing individual counseling as well as leading educational programs in marriage enrichment, and child education.

For one year she was persuaded by the Counseling Department of Concordia College to teach a class in counseling. This experience was both satisfying and challenging to her. She tried out for acting in a play at the FM Community Theater, and was given a part in a production. She volunteered to be on duty in the surgery waiting room at St. Lukes as a counselor on site as needed. She also served as a member of the ND Mental Health Counselors Association.

With all of her involvements she continues to be my best friend, and often my counselor.

7. The Gambling Disease

In the 1980's our county became enamored with gambling as the remedy for all of our financial needs. North Dakota had legally forbidden gambling since the days when it was first made illegal in the Dakota Territory days after it had ravaged society in those days.

Now it came to the people of North Dakota as a way to meet the charitable needs of the state, by introducing local game cards, and bingo sites. Charitable Gaming was to be the answer to all of our charitable needs. The idea wouldn't sell after several attempts before the voters, but the pressure began to build. Several of us were involved in anti-gambling education efforts. Governor Arthur Link was dead set against any form of gambling, envisioning what it could do to the social structure of North Dakota. Governor Link and I teamed up to make several presentations across the state urging defeat of the issue in the coming election. With all of the effort that was put into the battle against the issue it passed, and at this time we have all kinds of gambling opportunities and our issues still have needs. The State has also become a part of the national lottery.

Lutheran Social Services is the only agency in the state that is equipped to deal with Addictive Gambling, and they do not have enough personnel to meet all of the problems. The state's charities still have to make their general appeals for operating funds. Economic studies seem to indicate that the impact of gambling on the economy of North Dakota that any gains made are offset by the many societal issues the presence of gambling generates. I recognize I have a rather jaundiced view of the whole scene. I do foresee that the problems raised might have to accelerate to the place where society will recognize what it is doing to itself, as they did once in our past before anything positive will be done about it.

As indicated earlier, retirement has opened many avenues of life that were not available to us when we were employed full time.

Another such activity that was now opened to me in a new way was hunting possibilities.

As a boy my Dad and I had a few times of hunting together, although his work didn't allow much time for that. I was able to do bird hunting during my High School years with friends. Then followed a hiatus on hunting possibilities until I was assigned to the Fairmount parish. One of the limitations of being Pastor in this regard is that on week-ends when most other people are free to go hunting, a Pastor is not.

Friend Pastors Bernard Curtis and Max Brown made occasional trips to Fairmount so we could hunt that country together. There were pheasants, but only cock pheasants could be shot.

One of our party, on this particular day, made the mistake of downing a hen pheasant. The feelings of all but one of our party was to leave it for the foxes. That one insisted he was going to take it home and eat it. He pushed it up on the top of the glove compartment of my car. As we traveled the rough country trails the pheasant was jiggled enough that soon her legs would be dangling down under the dash in obvious presence. Again I asked the question, "Is it worth it?" My friend insisted that it was and kept pushing the bird back up above the glove compartment. We did make it safely home without encountering a Game Warden. I never had the nerve to ask my friend if he really enjoyed eating that bird.

Among the friends we developed during my time on the District were Jesse and Lorraine Anderson. They were devoted members of the Enderlin United Methodist Church. They lived on a beautiful little farm north of Enderlin along the Maple River. Their farm was the home of many deer. Together we worked out a once a year outing at the beginning of deer season in early November. We looked forward to our time with the Andersons. Deer hunting there was a cinch, and I usually had my deer within an hour or two of hunt start.

One memorable year was when, on our outing, we drove into the farmstead of a deserted farm that Jess's son-in-law farmed. I had just purchased a new Marlin deer rifle and was anxious to try it out. As we drove into the farmstead in Jesse's old pickup there were three deer standing before the garage door looking at us. I got out of the pickup quietly, leveled the barrel over the hood of the pickup, zeroed in on my scope, and pulled the trigger. Just a "click"! Thinking it must be a dud of a shell I ejected it and tried once more. "Click" The third time: "Click"

I finally realized that the gun was on safety. With my old gun when it was on safety you couldn't even pull the trigger. With this one the trigger pulled, but the safety put a barrier so the hammer wouldn't hit the shell. We both watched helplessly as the three deer turned and sauntered slowly off into the shelter belt. Was that a look of disdain on their faces? Fortunately, within about two hours I had another opportunity, and got my deer.

That evening we and the Andersons went in to Enderlin to have dinner with some friends from years back – Jack and Verna Armstrong. As I shared the story of our hunt with them the place was filled with guffaws.

 Two days later I received the following poem in the mail:

Ode to a deer

Standing still in morning light,
A deer, no thought of headlong flight,
Not seeing the danger lurking near,
Nor hearing, "Ah ha, I've got my deer!"
A look at last observed the threat.
Eyes widen with dread – and yet
Eyes look again with a sly deer wink.
The deer thinks, as deer do think
"I'm safe! – no danger to my ticker!"
"I know that guy! – he's Dave the clicker!"
– Jack Armstrong, Poet

Before we left Fargo First Church we took advantage of another exchange pulpit trip to England.

This time we ended up in the western Midlands, at Kingswinford, England, near Birmingham. Geoff and Margaret

Rushton, from the Kingswinford church took our place at First United Methodist Church in Fargo. Before Geoff left his parish in England he lined up a tight schedule of visitations, studies, services. Our days were so filled with activities that it was difficult finding time to make scenic trips into the countryside around Kingswinford. The advantage, of course, was that we had more opportunity to get to know people.

The parish in Fargo is especially quiet during the summer months because many from the Fargo area either own cabins in Minnesota, or arrange to spend some time at a cabin. Therefore about the only expectations we could make of Geoff was serving the Sunday services and being on call for emergencies. This didn't stop Geoff and Margaret from putting almost 5,000 miles on our automobile as they visited the country, including the Rocky Mountains.

One of the most meaningful dimensions of this trip was that the tour group met us at Kingswinford and spent two nights in local homes before leaving as a Tour Group to visit some of the sights of England around Kingswinford, and then we settled in on the early Methodist and Wesley sites in London before taking off for home.

One of the suspense filled experiences of the trip began with our visit to York Cathedral. The group had decided to climb the steps to the top of the Cathedral tower from which one could see the wide countryside. One of group was Ila Telkamp from Brookings, SD. Before we left for the tower tour Ila announced that she would stay below rather than do the climb. Ila was 89 years old at the time. As Jane and Ila visited on a nearby bench until the rest of us could all join together again, Ila announced to Jane: "You know I have an inoperable aneurism in my head!" No we didn't know that! For Jane and I the nature of the tour activities changed from that moment on, and we breathed a deep sigh of relief when we put her on a plane from Minneapolis to Sioux Falls, SD. But bless her heart, Ila lived over three more years after her return home.

Retirement was to allow us more such travel opportunities. Just the two of us returned to England one more time, traveling on our own with public transportation, and visiting friends we had made on previous trips.

About this time we had a letter from the Farden Township Board, where our cabin was located. We had had some struggles with the Board before over the Township right-of-way which divided our property – a road that didn't go anyplace but on our property.

I met with the Board at their Township Hall near Bemidji in March. They announced that they had looked over our building site, and we had built our living room overhanging the right-of-way by about three feet. They gave us two alternatives: either tear down our living room, or make it smaller so it would fit, or we could have the right-of-way re-surveyed so it would swing over the necessary three feet to make our living room "legal." I tried all of the arguments I could think, bearing down on the reality that there was no road on the right-of-way and furthermore there could be no road made beyond our property line.

There being no resolution by any arguments I could make we hired a surveyor at no small cost to move the course of the right-of-way. Then we had to remove several trees, and hire a bulldozer to form up a new roadbed because the new alignment would have put the right-of-way about three feet over the edge of the ridge. So much for the fun of trying to negotiate with a Township Board. Someone gave me the insight that Township Boards are no longer necessary in today's government set-up, but they become wonderful places for small people to be elected so they can feel big! I am inclined to believe there is something to that!.

I must admit, however, that the change has been good for us. It allows more sunshine to reach our cabin and gardens than could do that before.

Time to Volunteer

"Only a life lived for others is a life worthwhile"
– Albert Einstein

Another open door that retirement allowed us was to get involved in a variety of volunteer experiences that were enriching and exciting. Since we didn't yet have permanent housing we decided that for the time being we would spend as much of the year as we could at the Haven, and divide the winters between times spent with the family and volunteering for ventures in the south where it was warm.

Our first inquiry was for opportunities to volunteer at McCurdy School in Espanola, NM.

McCurdy School had been established as a boarding school in 1912 by the Evangelical United Brethren Church. The EUB Church and the Methodist Church had since become one – The United Methodist Church.

The School originally had dormitory units for housing students from the surrounding area. It had a farm with poultry and livestock so it was practically self-supporting as far as food was concerned. There had been a large garden and a large apple orchard. The School had been established for Elementary through High School students. Although the area is predominantly Catholic, the Catholic church, recognizing the quality and availability of education at McCurdy, provided only elementary education for their own children, and encourages the others to attend McCurdy High School.

As we approached Espanola the first year we volunteered, when we got to Santa Fe we were engulfed in a raging blizzard. We questioned whether we could even continue. As we came to a service station we stopped to make inquiry. The advice was to continue slowly because as we descended the hill into the valley we would leave the blizzard behind. They were right.

We joined about twenty other volunteers. We were housed in what had been the dormitories. The dining hall fed us faithfully. No students stayed on campus anymore. There were about 250 students enrolled, in all grades. Our responsibilities covered the gamut from mentoring students to care of the buildings and grounds. Jane served as an associate teacher for the 5th and 6th grade class. I worked mainly with the office, typing up lesson plans and keeping a record of activities. I also did some mentoring of High School students. One of the greatest needs was help with mathematics. I quickly discovered they were using a different method in mathematics than I was familiar with – but I told them "I can always get the correct answer." It was a learning experience in both directions.

We spent three months at McCurdy, and then started making our way back to the Dakotas and Minnesota. In all we were to spend three winters at McCurdy School. I have great admiration for the job they are doing in a varied population of different backgrounds, and different economic levels.

Our next adventure was with Heifer Project International near Little Rock, Arkansas.

After World War II a young farmer from Ohio named Dan West, a member of the Church of the Brethren, was serving as a "cowboy" taking cattle aboard ship from the United States to the war torn countries of Europe. His intent was to see that children could have milk to drink. On one of his trips the idea had come to his mind that these children did not need a cup of milk, they needed a cow. Back in the U.S., and now in Indiana, he began to talk to farmers he knew in the Church of the Brethren, and together they came up with forming a "Heifer Relief Committee." The concept grew and the practice grew until in 1944 the organization "Heifers for Relief" was formed. The concept was to ship pregnant heifers overseas, with the stipulation that the recipients were to pass on the first calf to another needy family.

Since then the organization has flourished and expanded. Today Heifer Project offers all sorts of possibilities: cattle, sheep, pigs, chickens, geese, bees, and many other things. The idea is still the same: the recipients are to pass on offspring to someone else.

In 1995 Jane and I spent three months at the headquarters near Little Rock. Jane spent most of her time in the office, shipping out educational and promotional materials. Together with another volunteer friend, David Krewson, we finished off a small building that is now used for on-site educational needs. The compound near Little Rock is a ranch that includes most of the creatures involved in the outreach. That in itself was a wonderful experience. One could wake up one morning either hearing sheep bleat, or a camel bellow.

The Organization has received many awards for the excellent work it is doing, and the development of the concept that has done wonders in transforming communities around the world.

Our fellowship with the folk there was so joyous an experience. We went back another winter for three months of service.

Our friendship with old Navy Buddy Jack Hood in Rock Hill, SC continued through the years. We made several trips to visit Jack, and his wife Marjorie, and appreciated their friendship so much.

Hurricane Hugo had struck the South Carolina coast in September of 1989. The devastation was severe and widespread. Our United Methodist Church was very involved in reconstruction operations, so they would advertise for volunteers to come down to help restore housing for many folk who were still not back in their homes. Jane and I decided to sign up to do this for a winter stay in 1996.

In September of 1995, we had a call from the United Methodist office responsible for such volunteer ventures. They had an urgent request. Instead of working on housing reconstruction would we consider being on-site managers of a small homeless shelter in North Charleston. Their Manager had suddenly quit and the local community was trying to keep the place in operation by themselves.

The very thought of being involved in a homeless shelter was rather a daunting thought to us, but as we considered it we called friend volunteers from before, Dave and Bev Krewson in Toledo Ohio. "If we were to accept this responsibility would you be willing to join us there?" We talked about it for a while, the Krewsons considered, and then called back to say they would come. So we agreed to accept the opportunity for new experience it offered. It was one of those "once in a lifetime" experiences, but don't need to have another like it. We drove to South Carolina, and visited the our friends, Jack and Margie Hood in Rock Hill, SC before heading down to North Charleston.

The Shelter was established by a group of churches from North Charleston. They called it The Good Neighbor Center. The managing Board had arranged to rent an old motel that was built at the conclusion of WWII. It was located across from the old Navy Yards. The Center used only the ground floor. Six rooms had been prepared, each housing 6-7 guests. There were also two large bedrooms that we and the Krewsons occupied. During one of our months there we recorded 600 Person-nights.

Five of the occupants were given on-going responsibilities: Collie, maintenance; James, cook; Dorothy, office help; Derek, housekeeping; Diana, laundry. We soon discovered that many of the occupants were mentally ill. I think ALL of the so-called responsible persons were mentally ill. We had one incident when James was chasing one of the other staff around the facility with a butcher knife! It soon became obvious that we and the Krewsons would have to stick to the job 24/7 for at least the first month. After that we would take turns going off the campus for short trips.

The Chair of the Interchurch Committee was Martha Knight, a local school executive. Martha had an indomitable spirit. She would check in with us most every day, coming in the door cheerily with the greeting: "Merry Christmas." Martha was the one who kept things humming, and with the chaos at the Center she had to deal also with the chaos within the committee. Two other members of the Board left indelible impressions on us: Achim Daffin, a young, energetic Presbyterian Pastor, completely dedicated to making the experiment proceed; and Inez Mitchum, an elderly Saint, who served the enterprise with strength and vigor that seemed to come from a divine source. These three persons really kept the Shelter moving along.

Working with the mentally ill help was difficult, but together with these there were wonderful people there who, down on their luck, were working hard to save enough to get back on their own again. One was a handsome, young black man who worked as an orderly in a nursing home. His face shone like the sun on the day he came to us and said goodbye, announcing that he had saved enough money to move into an apartment on his own.

Our cook, James, was a small black man who did a fair job of cooking, but he was always complaining about something He wanted to get to New Orleans. I worked all the angles I could until I finally obtained a one-way bus ticket for him to get to New Orleans. I heard afterward that when I walked out of the room after presenting him with the ticket, he cussed me "up one side and down the other."

But we survived, and we are grateful for the experience. It has given us a much greater appreciation of some of issues that many homeless in our country today are struggling with.

Knowing that the day would come when we could no longer sponge off the children, or escape to volunteer projects somewhere in God's creation, we had visited with Steve Stoner, a Realtor who was one of the movers and shakers at Fargo First Church. We told him we were interested in a small condominium , all on one floor, with an attached garage, and a real fireplace. After our sojourn at the homeless shelter we stopped to see the Hoods again before heading north. While we were there Stoner called us and said he had exactly what we wanted. He described it to us, but we weren't willing to buy it sight unseen. He replied: "Now I have an idea what you're looking for, and there will be others available."

When we returned to Fargo there was another unit available in the same unit he had first called us about. We looked it over. Just what we wanted. So arrangements were made to buy our condominium at South 35th Street, Number 102. The condo is within three blocks of a super market, and four blocks to a hardware store and bank and five blocks from the post office. What more could we want!

Now we can really dance the dance of life!

All of our married life, since we began our ministry at Fairmount in 1953, we have lived in houses owned by the churches we served. In the United Methodist Church they are generally called "parsonages," places for the "parson" to live. In our ministry we were very fortunate in the parsonages provided for us. I am of the opinion that as the Cabinet considered the size of our family (ultimately 9!) considering our appointment may have been partly decided by which church had a large enough parsonage to house us all! In my experience through the years I have seen some parsonages that were hardly livable. In recent years our Annual Conference has established standards that must be met in a parsonage before a pastor is appointed. Upkeep of the parsonage is in the hands of the local Board of Trustees. Their care can vary from excellent overseeing to almost complete disregard. We were fortunate in the Boards of Trustees responsible for the parsonages in which we lived.

Now we were faced with a new adventure: actually owning the house in which we live. It was an exhilarating experience. What fun we had furnishing our new "space."

During the Fall and Winter of 1994-95 Jane and I volunteered to serve as mentors of children at Jefferson School in northwest Fargo. This area of the city is basically an area for lower middle class homes. As the rental is more reasonable there than in many parts of the city, a lot of families from other lands were predominant. The Principal of the school indicated to me that they were dealing with children of seventeen different languages. Can you imagine the difficulty it must have been to communicate with parents of the children. We were responsible for meeting with individual children after school to do some reading with them, and to help them with their studies as best we could. It was a very wonderful experience for us. The children were so appreciative of anything one did to help them. They especially enjoyed our reading to them, and our listening to them as they read to us.

Later in the Spring the Fargo School Board presented us with a recognition certificate of our "outstanding volunteer work" at Jefferson School.

We spent the month of March 1997 in Chandler, AZ with our daughter Jeanne. She was in the Air Force, stationed at Luke AFB at that time. It was so good to have the break of warm weather.

Since many folk from the Fargo area winter in Arizona we were privileged to spend time with many of them. While there we had two especially exciting experiences.

The first was while we were visiting friends at Prescott, AZ. In 1995 two amateur astrologists discovered a comet that had not been seen before. It was named after the two men – Hale-Bopp – and the word was out that it was about to make an appearance again. So together with our friends we headed to the outskirts of the city, and as we gazed at the night sky, there it was! It was our first time to see a comet at all, but what a thrill to see a newly discovered one.

The second experience was one that only I could enjoy as a retired veteran. Jeanne's Air Force unit was one whose main mission was to re-fuel planes in the air. With my Air National Guard connections Jeanne was able to schedule me on a re-fueling flight. The anticipation grew as I boarded the monster plan equipped to do the job. When we were in the proper space for re-fueling I sprawled on my stomach in the rear turret and watched the operation take place. What a thrill to see what appeared from my vantage point, that slender needle of a fuel pipe reach out and make contact with the A-10 they were refueling. In but a short time the operation was completed.

After we left Chandler, AZ the end of March we left for a three week trip to England, on our own, making our way from one end of that enchanted island to the other by means of BritRail. We planned our own journey, according to our own schedule, visiting friends and places from northern Scotland in the north to the scenic areas of Cornwall in the southwest. England has always had a fascination for both of us, and we wanted to make this last sentimental journey.

The year 1997 was a year of losing many of our dear friends, making us painfully aware of the mortality of human life. Richard Teichmann, who had been a part of our life from our years at Faith Church in Fargo when Dick was going to college, to our years of ending ministry at Fargo First Church when he served as our Associate Pastor. In the middle of a North Dakota blizzard Dick was out blowing snow with his snow blower, and in the typical spirit of Dick, when he finished his own sidewalk and driveway, he went on to do his neighbor's. He died on the job.

He and his wife Joan, some years before, had spent a few days at our cabin on Little Wolf Lake, and while there had purchased lots from Louis Zopf just down the ridge form us. They had built a cabin there, and had only a few years to enjoy it as a family.

We also said goodbye to boyhood friend, Durward Koll, and his wife Dorothy. Dorothy had been in a nursing home for some time after a series of small strokes. Dur had some health problems too, but his death was sudden and unexpected about five weeks after Dorothy's.

In the midst of all the losses of the year it was a real celebration of the year when our daughter Chris attained her PhD in Educational Psychology.

Our winter of 1998 was pretty much a duplicate of the year before: we mentored students at Jefferson School, and then we drove south to spend the month of March with Jeanne in Chandler, AZ. We decided that this year, from Chandler, we would head east to spend some time with the Hoods in Rock Hill, SC. We were able to visit good friends along the route over to South Carolina. This was enjoyable. But there was a scary part of the trip. As we were going through Kentucky and Tennessee a weather system of tornadoes stalked our journey all the way. We kept track of their path by continually listening to small radio stations along the way. The tornadoes left a path of destruction along their way, but fortunately we managed to miss them all. It was a relief to arrive safely in South Carolina, just in the height of the azalea blooming season.

This was the year we legally formed a Limited Partnership with our children relative to the Haven Property. Every summer, as we gather during our annual Family Week, we have a business session during which we carry out the business of the partnership. One final item of each year is to put the question: "Are we wanting to sell this property at this time?" So far the resounding answer has been: "No!" One cannot help project one's thinking down the years, when we are no longer a part of the picture, and wonder what the future of the Haven will be.

In June it became apparent that my older sister Perne was no longer able to manage on her own in her home. She had one daughter who had enough problems in their own family situation. We looked into assisted living situations in Devils Lake, and found one that was very pleasant and that Perne was willing to enter. In a short time she sold her home to a neighbor, and with some of our wider family's help were able to clear out the house and get Perne settled in the center. She was there for about five years before her death. This move for her was a great relief for me because she would not always remember her medications, and other things that needed to be done.

I was grateful for the excellent care she received there.

Sometime in the Spring son Jon called us with "an offer you can't refuse"! That should always be a warning sign. The emu industry was just beginning to emerge. The emu is a large bird, similar to the ostrich, a native of Australia. The commercial value of the emu is in raising them for their oil, which is a very "gentle" oil which is used for a lot of things: medications, lotions, cosmetic notions. Jon had an opportunity to buy a choice pair of chicks to begin his own emu operation. He had plenty of room in the old barn on their farmstead. He had the time to put into it. So we anteed up a financial assist and the industry was launched. Jon served on several boards and agencies to promote the projects, but for the most part it didn't take off. I think they needed to have someone full time on the promotion end of things. After a few years it was obvious that as far as the "Knecht" operation was concerned it wasn't going any place. It appears that the money was made by those who first promoted the possibilities and sold the chicks.

The World is Our Parish

"All the world is our parish." – John Wesley, founder of Methodism

We were enjoying the peace and quiet of our summer at the Haven when we received an unexpected phone call from friend David Wu. David, a native of China, was now working for the General Board of Global Ministries in New York. I had the privilege of marrying David to Shirley Preszler, who had been a missionary of our church in Korea for many years. David greeted me warmly, and after we had taken a couple of minutes to catch up on our personal activities, he said something like this: "Dave, we are looking for a special person to undertake a special project for the Board of Global Ministries." I remember my initial response: "David, why me? " He assured me that Jane and I had the qualities that fit their need precisely. So then he dropped the proposition. One of the missionaries in Lithuania was being transferred to another assignment, ad the missionary family who was to replace him would not complete their training until the end of the year. "Would you and Jane be willing to go to Lithuania for 3 ½ months to serve the parishes until the Markays could be in place?" My responsibility would be to serve three churches during that time. Jane's responsibility would be to help them plan and train in the area of Christian education. How could we refuse?

So in September we took off into the "wild blue yonder" to an adventure we could not even imagine, to an area of the world that was completely foreign to us, at a time when the behemoth of Stalinist Russia was just withdrawing from the European scene, and the little nation of Lithuania was trying to find out who she was after 50 years of Soviet rule.

When the Soviets took over the country all vestiges of Lithuania as an independent country were done away with. The official language became Russian. The Lithuanian language was not to be spoken at all, and all signs of the old Lithuania were obliterated. The Methodist Church was not allowed to worship, and all of its properties were confiscated. The Roman Catholic church could continue in a limited way, as could some Baptist churches.

The largest congregation I was responsible for was in Kaunas, a large city. After months of legal battles they had succeeded in getting back their old building. The Soviets had turned it into a recreation hall for troops, so it had been badly used. The congregation at Kybarti was 60 miles southwest of Kaunas. The original Methodist property had not been returned, but the congregation had refurbished an old house which served as its Sanctuary. This was true of the congregation at Pilviskai as well. The congregations had enthusiasm, and there were a lot of children. We were served by a young woman interpreter Jurate Klepsaite, and driven to our sites by Vitas, who had been a part of the system under the Soviets. We were housed in a small but pleasant apartment in Kaunas.

A lot of fear was still evident. Most of our people were very poor. Some of them had had jobs under the Soviet system, but no longer did. Most of the older folk had received a small pension, but no longer received anything. The congregation had no experience in making their own decisions. I was working with them to set a time for the Christmas service in Kaunas, but they had no idea of how to come to a consensus. Jane and I led a conflict resolution workshop because there were persons with very divided opinions in the congregations. It was a birthing time for the small country, and the birth pangs were severe.

But we also met some wonderful, devoted Christian people, who had 'toughed it out' during the Soviet occupation. They hid the Bible, or parts of it at least, in their homes. They sang to themselves some of the old hymns they loved. The Lithuanian flag is a simple flag of three horizontal stripes: red, yellow, green. One woman told of keeping three strips of cloth hidden in her house, and on special occasions would lay them out on the table like a flag.

It was an unforgettable experience, and we will ever be grateful for the opportunity.

When it came time for us to leave, just after Christmas but before the New Year began, there were fears that we would not be able to fly out. The question was whether the computer systems could smoothly make the transition to a new century. But the day came and all went well.

With the new-found freedom we registered for an Elder Hostel in Florida in February. Theme of the Hostel was "Music in Nature; Nature in Music." We were exposed to some wonderful music, both instrumental and vocal, and to some of the natural resources around the camp where we were housed. We were a bit shocked on finding snakes in our cabin when we moved in, but we were assured they were harmless. We drove on many new an scenic highways which allowed us to visit friends both down and back. Jane had never been to Florida before. I had only been to the area around Jacksonville in the north when I was stationed there for a while in WW II.

Another beautiful experience was a trip to the bed and breakfast "B & B - 2217 Melstad Place. Just outside of Mountain, ND. Mountain is an old Icelandic community, very evident in the people and even the buildings of the little community. The surroundings of the old house in which we lived were well cared for, and profuse with flowering plants. A large temporary shelter was up on the large lawn on one side of the house. We asked our hostess about it. She said the community had just concluded a celebration of their Iceland Republic Day, June 17. Iceland became a Republic in 1944. She went on to say that the President of Iceland had been present at the Mountain festival, and that we had slept in the same room in which he had slept. "We did change the bedding!" she reported with a wide smile on her face.

On the 8th of April I had the honor of uniting our third daughter, Jeanne, with Duane Scheffler, in holy matrimony. The wedding took place in the community building of the city of Woodbury, MN.
The newlyweds drove off from the wedding site in Duane's old vintage automobile.

The year 2000, in addition to be the beginning of a new century, was one of the most tightly packed year of activities I think we have ever experienced.

Upon our return from Lithuania we were asked to make many presentations about our experience there. Through our presentations we were able to make the people of the Dakotas aware of the mission need in the tiny country. In years following First Church in Fargo alone made many work trips of a week or two to assist the young church in getting their feet on the ground.

Next door to us in the apartment where we had lived in Kaunas was a family who had a 17 year old son still at home. We made acquaintance with Kestas first of all through our mutual interest in stamp collecting. I was able to funnel a lot of U.S. stamps to him which really swelled his collection. He would stop by our apartments some evenings and we taught him to play Rummy and Kings in the Corner. Before we left Lithuania we made arrangements for him to come to America to visit us. A part of the experience was to be chance for him to address the United Methodist Youth of the Area at their Leadership Training Camp at Lake Poinsett in South Dakota. We tried to plan as many experiences as we could to expose him to American culture and people. I remember vividly the first time I took him to one of our Super Markets. We just stepped inside the door, and seeing shelf after shelf of a variety of foods his eyes opened wide and all he could say was: "Oh, God!" We continue to keep in contact with Kestas who is married now, and has two children. After attempting to find several types of work he has finally signed up for the military and that seems to be a stabilizing force in his life.

Son Timothy disappeared off our family "radar" for about 13 months. We had absolutely no contact with him, or way of getting in contact with him. We knew he had been in the Phoenix area the last we had heard from him, so we called the Arizona State Patrol to see if they had any record of him. We thought of the possibility of him dying in some way. The State Patrol had a record of his being arrested once in Phoenix for "disturbance of the peace," but that was all. The only thing we could do was play the waiting game. We finally got a call from Tim from California. He was ready and would soon work his way home.

Our friend Richard Teichmann had died suddenly two years before while fighting snow in a blizzard. Joan and the family were not visiting their lake property next to us at Little Wolf Lake, and the cabin was beginning to deteriorate. I said to Joan: "I recognize it has been difficult for you to come regularly to the cabin, but I am concerned about its physical care. Have you ever thought of selling it? If so would you please give us first chance to buy?" She assured me she would. Shortly after that she listed the property with a Bemidji realtor, and after a while came to me to say she was ready to sell. My response: "I recognize that I will not be able to pay what you think it is worth. My concern is that the sand point well is no longer in working condition, and that there is no permanent sewage disposal unit in existence, so that will take considerable money to meet those requirements, but let me make an offer." So we tried to estimate what the total cost to us might be. I finally offered $11,500 for the cabin and a couple of pieces of furniture she wished to dispose of. She accepted the offer, and on July 11, 2000 we signed the papers of purchase.

This was the winter of the big Fargo flood, when the city came close to being entirely abandoned because of the rapidly rising water from the confluence of the Red and the Cheyenne Rivers. FEMA was recommending that the city be evacuated. Our Mayor Wallacher was not willing to do that, and fortunately the city miraculously fought the rising water with sand bags and dikes and the city was saved. Nevertheless it caused hardship for many people, and months of restoring things to order again. Now the City and surrounding area is in a massive planning process to prevent this kind of event to disrupt things again. It will be months, perhaps years, however until all parties are in agreement on a plan and finances are in place to realize it.

My older sister Perne, who lived in Devils Lake, was in and out of nursing homes for several months and it became clear she was no longer able to care for her own needs. The family finally convinced her to take up residence in the Heartland Care Center. When she was settled in she enjoyed the facilities and the people she got to know there. It was a great relief to her, and to all the family. She was able to live at the Care Center for the next two years, until her death in July of 2002.

This was also the year when historic Wesley College was sold to the University of North Dakota. It wasn't feasible to keep the college going because of financial changes in the area, and the changes in curriculum structure at the University. Basically the University established its own religion department, and music offerings, that replaced those that Wesley College had offered.

During this year Jane took up renewed interest in watercolors and oils. She had definitely inherited the talent from her family background. Her Grandma Sheldon had produced some awesome paintings in her lifetime. Jane enjoyed the hobby although she discovered she had difficulty finding time. Through the years Jane has produced some fine paintings. Furthermore she has passed on the gift to son Jon who is very involved in the art scene in Mankato, MN.

As summer drew to a close Jane and I heard about another Elderhostel in South Carolina, so we called them to inquire. The topic was to be "Southern Mansions and Anti-bellum Homes." I asked the secretary whether we were too late to register. She chuckled and replied, "No, actually you are the first ones to register." So we registered. Then we called our friends Jack and Margie Hood in Rock Hill and asked if they would be interested in going. They were. We planned a driving trip down that included a stop to visit several friends on the way. At the last we picked up the Hoods and went to the site of the Elderhostel, at the Bonnie Doone Plantation between Charleston, SC and Savannah, GA.

On our arrival we were delighted to learn that the we and the Hoods would be housed in the Plantation House itself. When they took us to our quarters Jane and I were to be located in the "Master's Bedroom," and the Hoods in the "Mistress' Bedroom," both delightfully furnished and massive in size. In typical Plantation tradition, apparently, the Master and the Mistress each had their own bedrooms, but they were joined by a passageway between the two rooms through the closets! Some of the other attendants were housed in servant quarters rooms which hardly allowed enough room to get to the side of the bed! We took some kidding about that.

During the Elderhostel we were exposed to the culture and music of the times, and made some short trips to nearby villages and plantations to see other examples of the life of those anti-bellum days. What elegance had been built on the backs of the slave culture.

During this year we experienced the death of many dear friends and family members to. We also experienced the divorce of two of our closest friends – a real shock to us. It seemed as though we had assumed that anyone within our circle of friends were as devoted to each other as we are. How often we go through life making assumptions that we have no foundation for making! To learn the lesson that each person must have the space to make the choices that they choose to make is often difficult for our minds to grow into.

Life Is Change

"In family life, love is the oil that eases friction, the cement that binds closer together, and the music that brings harmony." – Eva Burman

The year 2001 was a big one in our marriage: we celebrated 50 years together. Who would have thought that we could have fifty years of married life. To celebrate we decided to host the family at a commercial resort. Although we would have had everything the resort offered at our own Haven, we realized that we would have more freedom there: freedom from meal making, and freedom from the usual chores that staying at the Haven would involve. We went to a local restaurant one evening for dinner. We could easily prepare snacks and luncheons at the resort. The family planned an entertaining afternoon recalling the events and the music of the fifties. Our grandchildren played a very important part of this. It was a great time to be together again.

In February we spent a month at the headquarters of Heifer Project International in Arkansas. Jane was involved in the promotion office sending materials out to various persons or organizations requesting them. Dave Krewson, with whom we had already been involved in other volunteer activities, and I were given the assignment of finishing off the interior of building that was to be devoted to the education of persons who came to the center to learn about Heifer Project. It was exciting to be living on the headquarters "ranch" for it housed examples of all of the creatures they made available in their program. One would awaken in the morning to the baaing of sheep, the call of cattle, the grunt of camels and a myriad of other creatures.

Our days were full of family activities as the families grew in involvement in their own outreach, and in number. How thankful we are for each of them.

The next two years saw some fundamental changes in our family's lives: the death of my sister Perne, of Allan Church, Ryan's father, and Roy Schaar, Scott's father. My brother-in-law, James Abrahamson was no longer able to care for himself, so was placed in Manor Care assisted living in Fargo. Jeanne's Air National Guard company was sent to Kuwait as a follow up to "Operation Storm. That proved to be both an exciting experience and a somewhat scary experience for her.

Jane and I drove to Evanston, Illinois so we could attend the 50th Anniversary of my graduating class from Garrett. It was great to see some old friends from those days. The campus, however, had made some changes that were necessary but disappointing. The original main building of the campus had an open visiting and reading area on the first floor. It was an inviting place to just hang out. That area had now been divided into smaller rooms for various offices and meeting rooms required by the additional enrollment. The parking area, which had been a free, and available parking area at most any hour of the day, was now an assigned parking area, with a very limited area available for visitors. Lake Michigan was no longer visible from the Garrett Campus. Northwestern University had barged in millions of tons of earth extending their campus far out into the Lake. But being on the campus brought back a flood of pleasant memories of the three years we had spent there.

Another year (2004) and a host of changes in our lives that impact us in some exciting ways. Early in the Spring Jane and I took a month-long journey to South Carolina and back, visiting many friends along he way. We travelled over 5,000 miles on that venture. As a part of it we stayed in a Time Share experience, and in the process put out big money to join with the BlueGreen Time Share Vacation program. Jeanne was sent to Germany to the US Air Base near Frankfurt. Jane and I went over to visit there for about 10 days – a beautiful area just on the edge of the Black Forest territory. Other major changes in family life: Jane's sister Joanne and her husband Lloyd Reynolds, both retired from teaching in Washington and Montana and chose Bozeman MT for their home. Laurie's husband, A.J. Kluver, who had taught school for years, had responded to a call to ministry in the Evangelical Lutheran Church. He had begun his training at Luther Seminary in the Twin Cities, and was experiencing his internship with a parish in Staples, MN.

In the Spring of 2005 I was asked if I would serve as interim pastor for Friendship UMC in south Fargo from March until Annual Conference in June. The congregation, which was a relatively new congregation, was being slowly smothered by a Pastor who was gradually offending one after another of his congregation. What he was doing was obvious to the Annual Conference but given the atmosphere of the times in which we live it was not easy to remove him from this appointment so the congregation could move on. It was undoubtedly the most difficult assignment I had ever been given because it seemed like the process of deterioration was so far along that it couldn't be reversed. The ultimate result was that the congregation, as it was, had to be terminated and its membership transferred to another congregation. As is so true in some life situations, however, the death of that congregation gave rise to a new ministry that is thriving and meeting an important need of persons who in recovery from one catastrophe in their lives or another.

Later in that year we were able to put our membership in Blue Green to good use. We took a vacation at Boyne Mountain, a ski resort near Traverse City, MI. It was off-season for skiing and we pretty much had the place to ourselves. It was cherry blossom time in northern Michigan, and the country side was beautiful. We also got to visit Don and Mary Sheldon, who retired there, and Marge Lempke and her family, the family of my old Navy buddy, Harry Lempke.

Later in the summer we again took advantage of our Blue Green membership, and spent a week at Big Sky Montana, another famous ski resort, but out of season. Jane's brother Bill and his wife Marlene accompanied us on this trip. We were also close to her sister and husband in Bozeman, so it was a wonderful family time.

In August our tenth Grandchild was born – Aubrey Allison Knecht – child of Jon and Amy. Since she came quite a while after the previous grandchild, and since she is the only one who is a "Knecht" she has come into some favoritism, but she deserves it. Each of our grandchildren have brought a unique joy is their own special way.

More travel marked the year 2006. We made another trip to Rock Hill and Charleston SC, and stayed in a unique Blue Green property in downtown Charleston, giving us all kinds of viewing opportunities within walking distance. We took Jane's brother Bill, and wife Marlene to San Antonio Texas for Bill to attend a reunion of his Air Force Company that he had served with in Germany. One of the exciting activities of this trip was an evening spent in the riverside development of the old city of San Antonio. We were able to get together also with an old college friend of Jane's who lives there, and she was able to guide us to other sites of the city.

When we came home to the Haven we decided there were places and friends in North Dakota that we had not seen for some time, so we planned a Circle Tour of North Dakota. North Dakota gets a lot of razzing by much of the rest of the nation, as a "vast area of nothing." But North Dakota has many beautiful spots and interesting people. Highlights of the trip were times in the western Badlands, and the village of Medora, the magic highway from New Town down to the hills of Kildeer, the rugged hills of the northeast corner with its deep gorges and forested hills.

Other outstanding events of this year: our purchase of Time Share properties with Spinnaker resorts, with our holding in Branson, MO; the death of Marty Thoen, father of daughter-in-law Amy; Son-in-law A.J. Kluver's call to serve the Bethany ELCA in Nevis, MN; the purchase of a new Apple Computer. For Jane, she was chosen as Jewel of the Year by the United Methodist Women of First UMC in Fargo.

Another beginning for me this year was the start of eyeball shots for my macular degeneration. My vision was slipping away from me. Dr. Andrew Jordan, my ophthalmologist started me on a regular treatment of injections of a new medicine called Avastin. When I was to receive the first one I was apprehensive, but now they are routine. It takes a day or two before vision returns to normal, but at least vision is maintained. I said to Dr. Jordan one day: What would it be like if this medicine were not available?" "You would be blind." was his curt reply. I am grateful for the wonderful medical possibilities we have here at home.

As more sign of our progressing age, Jane started treatment for glaucoma. It has been kept pretty well under control with eye drops. However she did have a cornea operation at the

University of Minnesota in St. Paul. This was to insert a drainage tube in her right eye to release the pressure.
The tube surgery went alright, but in the process when the stitches were removed a small segment of stitches were overlooked, and that created continual pain for her for about two years, until we insisted with her eye doctor that something was wrong. Upon inspection the remaining piece of stitch was discovered and she was referred to Dr. Keating at Essentia Health for cornea surgery. A new cornea was implanted but didn't take hold until with more radical medication. The cornea is now attached, but her vision in that eye has not improved significantly.

In September Jane and I and Lloyd and Joanne took an Alaskan Cruise. Jane and I drove out to Bozeman where the Reynolds live, and then we drove on to Seattle with them. There we boarded the Norwegian Star for a cruise of seven days. This was our first and only experience with a cruise. Although there were many hundreds of people of board, the facilities were spacious and we never felt pushed or crowded. Dining was fantastic. The young staff was very courteous and most helpful. There were many activities during the course of the cruise: lectures on the area, musical concerts, recreational and exercise possibilities. For the most part, however we simply enjoyed the beauty along the way and the uninterrupted time we had with Joanne and Lloyd. We made short stops at Ketchican, Juneau, Skagway and Prince Rupert. We made a trip out to the Mendenhall Glacier while in Juneau where we witness firsthand the rapid deterioration of the glaciers caused by the warming climate. As we sailed we watched many dolphins playing along the way. The disappointment of the trip is that we never saw whales.

While we were Mendenhall I was walking up the path to the Visitor's Center, and was met on the path by a black bear.

Apparently he was bored by all of the human visitors around, for he simply gave a quick glance and went on his way down the path.

Grandchildren continued to enter the college scene, and to graduate, and to get married. Now in the summer of 2008 it was the beginning of the Kluver's turn for marriages with the wedding of Kayla and Ryan Swenson. Down the line the Kluver marriages continued with Jacob and Lennea Asbury and Allison and Matthew Beach. Upon his graduation from High School in Alexandria, Benjamin followed his Grandfather's path and enlisted in the Navy. He is presently on the Machinist Mate path.

In these years son Jon has become very active in the art scene, particularly related to the Carnegie Art Institute in Mankato, MN. Twice he has had the Carnegie for a show of his own. He has sold many of his pieces, always with the comment of the art community that he puts too low a price on his work. He had begun his art sojourn while a student at Dakota Wesleyan University in Mitchell, South Dakota. It has been exciting to see him continue on this path through the years.
So we have definitely moved into the so-called "Golden Years" of our lives. Whoever pasted that title on the senior years must not have been there him/herself, because with increasing health problems, curtailed physical activities, the accelerated loss of friends and family to inevitable death or disability, it is sometimes far from a "golden" time of life. I have sometimes called them the "Silver Years" because silver is susceptible to tarnishing!

But on the other hand these years are so filled with goodness and grace as one watches family continue to grow, have families, take their responsible place in an ever-changing society. To persons of our age there are frightening signs ahead: the loss of solid moral foundations, the deterioration of the sense of the value of human life, the ever-increasing pace of time that seems to rob us of so much leisure and moments to enjoy beauty and wonder.

Our society seems to have adopted the value of having ever to INCREASE production, possession, impersonal communication. But one needs to accept the fact that every past generation has struggled with its own human problem – and the race is still here.

These years must be time to contemplate the in-built wonders of life.

With each discovery that is made in science and technology there are revealed more mysteries to be explored. I stand in awe and wonder of the beauty and complexity of life: our bodies, our capacities for relationships, the vastness and intricacy of the universe in which we have been born. I believe that is the essence of worship: awe and wonder before life.

A beautiful little book SMALL GRACES by Kent Nerburn would remind us that the fantastic riches of life are to be found in the "small graces" that mark every minute we draw breath. And this can lead us on to an acknowledgment of the Embracing Grace in which our whole beings exist.

It seems these latter years of life go by so quickly. It dazzles the mind, the speed with which changes are made in society, technology, the common patterns of existence.

Just within the last few months two mighty leaps have been made: the acceptance of gay and lesbian style of life, and the openness to the marriage of like-sexual persons. I think it was

Mark Twain who said, "I'd like to stay around to see how it all comes out." I must admit, somedays I'd rather not!

The Last Hurrah!

Said the little boy, "Sometimes I drop my spoon."
Said the old man, "I do that too."
The little boy whispered, "I wet my pants."
"I do that too." Laughed the little old man.

Said the little boy, "I often cry."
The old man nodded, "So do I."
"But worst of all," said the little boy, "it seems
Grown-ups don't pay attention to me."
And he felt the warmth of a wrinkled old hand.
"I know what you mean," said the little old man.
– Shel Silverstein

There is an ancient story told by the Venerable Bede (672-736 AD) about old King Edwin of Northumbria (England).

The King and his aide, Coifi, were considering the possibility of converting to Christianity. Coifi suggested, as one version of the story indicates, that life is like a sparrow. It flies out of the dark, stormy night, into an open window in the King's Grand Hall, where the King and his guests were having a great party with lights, and singing, and dancing. Then it flies on through the Hall and out into the darkness and cold through a window on the other side of the Hall. Coifu suggests that the Christian Faith offers a much brighter picture than that. The King ponders for a while, and then suggests that since the Christian Faith offers a much more cheerful ending to life, perhaps they should consider it.

There is no question that after all of the ages of the existence of humans as we know them, life is still a mystery. Where has it come from? Out of what primordial past has it emerged? Where is it going? What if anything lies ahead when the time of death arrives?

I am grateful that I was raised in a Faith in a God who holds the future. The mystery remains but I trust it to the Power which moves all that has been, is, and will be. As a Gospel song expresses it:

> *I know not what the future holds, but I know Who holds the future.*

There have been many times of doubt, bordering on unbelief in "anything," in my life. I have wrestled with these. But moving in the depth of my being comes an assurance strong and clear, and I put my trust in the assurance.

The vicissitudes of age have a way of pushing the question marks.

Robert Browning, the English poet, expressing the philosophy of an old Jewish Rabbi Ben Ezra, has the old Rabbi exclaim at one point:

> *Grow old along with me!*
> *The best is yet to be,*
> *The last of life, for which the first was made.*
> *Our times are in His hand*
> *Who saith "A whole I planned,*
> *Youth shows but half; trust God: see all, nor be afraid!"*

For many the so-called "Golden Years" are not very "golden." Limitations of mind and body plague so much of "the last of life" for so many. Jane and I are both experiencing the morass of dementia; Jane has been diagnosed as borderline

Alzheimer's – a diminishing of a portion of the brain for which at this time medical science has not found an answer. We are prepared to face these limitations together in the time that is given us, trying to focus on the old Rabbi's prescription: "Trust God: see all, nor be afraid."

There are some fundamental truths that life has spelled out for me clearly:

> Truth is always victorious over falsehood in the end.
>
> The fundamental nature of life is to trend toward wholeness and harmony, although it is often difficult to perceive this.
>
> Humans seem now to be at a crossroad in life where, making the right choices, life can evolve into a new level of "being" with powers of the spirit that have not yet been used, or even discovered, or we can destroy ourselves and our earth.
>
> Love is always victorious over hatred.
>
> There seems to be a "pattern" of life that offers peace and joy for our days, which I think Jesus pictured clearly in what we call the Sermon on the Mount. (Mt.5)

Some years ago folk singer Gordon Bok composed a song that has a haunting promise in its chorus:

> *"O my Joannie don't you know that the stars are swinging low,*
> *And the seas are rolling easy as they did so long ago.*
> *If I had one gift to give you I would tell you one more time*
> *That the world is always turning toward the morning."*

So the turning of our planet can bring us new assurance with the dawning of each new day.

Had I chance to live my life over there are some things I would choose differently I suppose. I am confident of God's forgiveness for times when I have "missed the mark." I have discovered that the treasure chest of God's Grace has no bottom.

During my Seminary days one of the outstanding theologians was Dr. Reinhold Niebuhr who taught for thirty years or more at Union Theological Seminary in New York. One of his often quoted statements sums the matter up for me in a masterful way:

> "Nothing worth doing is completed in our lifetime; therefore, we are saved by hope.
>
> Nothing true or beautiful or good makes complete sense in any immediate context of history; therefore, we are saved by faith.
>
> Nothing we do, however virtuous, can be accomplished alone; therefore, we are saved by love.
>
> No virtuous act is quite as virtuous from the standpoint of our friend or foe as from our own; therefore, we are saved by the final form of love, which is forgiveness.
>
> – Reinhold Niebuhr

What more can be said?

O Lord,
support us all the day long of this troublous life,
until the shadows lengthen, and the evening comes,
and the busy world is hushed,
and the fever of life is over, and our work is done.
Then, Lord, in thy mercy,
grant us a safe lodging, a holy rest,
and peace at the last.
Amen.

       – John Henry Newman, from the liturgy
              of the Church of England

ACKNOWLEDGEMENTS

I would like to dedicate this book to my beloved wife of over sixty-five years.

From the first time I spotted that beautiful, dark-haired, brown eyed young woman at a college youth gathering in the early 1950's, Lois Jane Sheldon took the top spot in my life, and has been the "music" that has inspired my "dance of life" since that day. The mother of our five beautiful daughters and two gifted sons, she has given herself completely to helping them develop meaningful and enjoyable lives, and to come to know the joy of contributing the unique gifts that are theirs to the community in which they live. Now in her eighties, with beautiful silver hair and bright brown eyes, Jane is still an inspiration to many.

My entire family is a continuing inspiration to me, and some of them have encouraged me to write a record of the life I have lived.

Our lives have been filled with wonderful friendships. To them we certainly owe so much of the "music" that has been a great part of our enjoyment of our days. Many of their lives are reflected in my story; they have helped to write the script of my own "symphony."

For special friend Don Homuth, reconnected in friendship after many years. I give special thanks. If it was not for his leading the way with the publication of his books, **Being Fargo** and **Becoming Fargo: Boy to Man**, and his encouragement that I could do the same, and his introducing me to Marc de Celle who has given freely of his professional competence, this project would not have happened.

I owe a special thanks to Marc de Celle, author of **How Fargo of You**. I was adrift in a sea of ignorance as far as publishing anything was concerned, and he offered his help freely. I thank him for his patience, and for his willingness, and hours of his own time and energy that he has devoted to help me get my manuscript off the ground and into a form that can take its place on someone's book shelf, and hopefully become somewhat of a guide and inspiration to their own journey.